UNLEASH THE SUPERNATURAL

Lenka Koloma

Copyright © 2018

All Rights Reserved

Disclaimer

Lenka Koloma is not a medical doctor and the contents of this book, website or any other media are for informational purposes only. The information does not constitute medical advice. It is not intended to substitute any professional medical advice, diagnosis or treatment. Always seek the advice of your health provider.

Book References

Osho, "Joy" The Happiness That Comes from Within
Herbert M. Shelton, "The Myth of Medicine"
Osho, "Freedom" The Courage to Be Yourself
J. Krishnamurti, "The First and Last Freedom"
Eckhart Tolle, "The Power of Now"
Christopher Ryan and Cacilda Jetha, "Sex at Dawn' The Prehistoric Origins of Modern Sexuality
Osho, "Sex Matters", From Sex To Superconsciousness
Osho, "Innocence, Knowledge and Wonder"

Dedication

This book is dedicated to my children. This includes my two most amazing biological sons Kai and Andre that I was privileged to bring into this life. They are an extension of me and everything I believe in and stand for. However, "my" children extend to all the other children of this world. This includes your children too.

    I dedicate this book to all children of this world that are our children. They deserve a different world, a world of peace and harmony. It is our duty as parents, aunts and uncles to create such a world for them. It is our legend we are leaving behind. It is now or never. Our children are our future and are our only hope. We need to build them into warriors of truth, love and compassion.

Acknowledgment

I am extremely grateful to my entire family who gave me space and unconditional support throughout my wild journey. They are the courageous people who put up with me and never gave up on me. They have always showered me with love and support.

I am thankful to life for all the pain, suffering and dark places I had to travel through to find my path and my light. On this path I found amazing teachers such as Osho and Dr. Herbert Shelton who have been instrumental in helping me to awaken and be able to see. Their knowledge and teaching continues to live through this book and my message. My gratitude extends to additional spiritual and science leaders such as Nikola Tesla, Albert Einstein, Jiddu Krishnamurti, Eckhart Tolle, Dr. Bruce Lipton, Dr. Joe Dispenza and Gregg Braden among the few.

PREFACE

Love is the language we all understand and speak. It is the language of all nations and every race. It is an universal language that needs no translation or instruction. It is the language of the Universe.

Unfortunately, through our technological evolution and knowledge seeking we have adopted an artificial language of the mind instead. This artificial language separated us from not only each other but our true selves as well. We accepted not loving ourselves as the norm and created a world of conflict and war as a result. We can feel, however, that something essential is missing. We can feel the big void and for that the search for the *forever bliss* is on.

I have encased my life's wild rollercoaster ride in this book. From being born handicapped, developing cancer to having a near death experience, the journey has not been easy at all. Through my misfortunate events and suffering, I learned to love my body and myself. I became responsive to what the Universe had to say to me. During times of emotional distress, asking yourself the question *"Who am I?"* and listening mindfully to the answers can do wonders to you and others.

Your sole existence is a proof that you have a purpose to fulfill in this world. It is time that you become the bravest of all because only you, with your trust in yourself, can conquer the world. Either you can be an antenna for positivity, which will lead you into becoming strong and independent, or you can become a receiver of negativity and fear, which will lead you into becoming weak and dependent.

Death, sex, family, love and faith, everything has been distorted by this outer world so brutally that you cannot see the reality or the actuality of these things. My life has taught me to listen to my own self and understand the fact that if I align myself with the Universe, I can do anything that I want, even when the whole world is against me.

In my book, I have tried to incorporate every aspect of life which needs amendments so that we can have a happy and joyful life. My sole purpose of writing this book is to make sure that everybody knows the secret to happiness. I hope you will find this book not only educational but also enlightening.

Contents

Dedication iii
Acknowledgment v
Preface vii

Chapter 1 Journey 1
Truth 1
Painful Beginning 5
Wisdom 9

Chapter 2 Purpose 13
Meaning of Life 13
False Self 16
Understanding Yourself 19

Chapter 3 Most Important Wealth 25
Climbing the Corporate Ladder 25
Race to Nowhere 27
Delusion of Becoming 31
Disease Delusion 34
Born Warrior 39
Winners Never Quit 43
Great Deception 45

Chapter 4 Freedom 51

Near Death Experience 56

Healing Miracle 61

Recipe for Miracles 66

The System 69

Chapter 5 Family 75

Infertility 75

Parents Worst Nightmare 77

The Art of Parenting 81

Education 88

Attachment 93

The Art of Dying 100

Nothing Ends 102

Chapter 6 Love 107

What Love Is Not 107

Tough Love 109

Life's Source 113

Contract on Love 116

Chapter 7 From Sex To Awakening 123

Unlike Animals 123

Desire 128

Sex Starvation 132

CONTENTS

Chapter 8 State Of Separation 139
Fear Programming 139
Pleasing Others 142
Addiction 150
Suicide 153
United We Stand 156

Chapter 9 Spirituality 161
Finding God 161
Living in Hell 167
United In Love 173
Deeper Truth 175

Chapter 10 Time Is Just An Illusion 181
Time Mystery 181
Memory Never Lived 186
Procrastination 188
Till Death Us Apart 189

Chapter 11 Alignment With The Universe 195
What You Are Looking For Is Looking For You 195
Living In A Bliss 198
Searching For Gold 202
What You Resist Persists 208
Self-Doubt 211

Resistance 213
Judgment 216
Working The Magic 218
Entitlement 221

About the Author..227

Chapter 1

JOURNEY

"To be beautiful means to be yourself. You don't need to be accepted by others. You need to accept yourself."

-Thich Nhat Hanh

Truth

You came to this world with a very specific purpose that only you can fulfill. It is only you and your sole magnificence that can complete this divine mission. You are the world's consciousness that manifests itself through your very being. This happens every fine moment of your life. Your energy and all that you bring is a special light this world has never seen before. You came here to shine this incredible light through your existence.

You are such a magnificent being. You are such a powerful being. You are bigger than anyone allowed you to believe. You are bigger than your mind allows you to think. You are bigger than your body allows you to feel. You are an unstoppable force this world is yet to see.

Everything happens for a reason. We do not always understand why things happen the way they do. We do not always know all they can possibly mean. But trust me when I tell you that there is always a bigger plan laid out. You are not some isolated element of this world. You are not out of its field of influence. You are an essential part of this world. You play a significant role.

The truth is that you have incredible powers to make miracles happen. In fact, if you look at it carefully you will realize that you are a miracle yourself. You are unlike anyone else on this planet and yet we are so alike. You are deeply connected with everyone else. Although we might appear apart, we are one.

This is to remind you and awaken your powers. This is to unleash the supernatural within you. You can be extremely happy or you can be extremely unhappy in your life. You can live an exciting life of ecstasy or mediocre life of monotony. The truth is you are free to choose. In order to choose, however, you have to be free. In order to be free you have to know the truth. In order to know the truth you have to be ready. You have to be ready to accept truth without judgment. You have to want the truth. There is no other way to infinite joy and bliss. Only truth can set you free. You want to be free. You want to finally let go and become the true you. Only truth can do this for you. Only truth can make you truly happy. That's the ultimate truth.

Truth is not easy. Truth is awfully difficult. Truth is not always welcome but it is always necessary. Truth is needed to dissolve hate and make room for love. Truth is love. Truth can never lie because it is fueled by unconditional love, the most powerful force of this Universe. Truth takes remarkable courage. Truth requires tremendous strength. Truth stands on the opposite side of fear. You have to be brave. You have to be fearless not only to speak your truth but also to be able to receive the truth. Truth is the ultimate emancipation. Truth is the highest level of sophistication.

Hearing truth will not always make you feel cozy and comfortable on the inside. The things you might feel are only triggers of unresolved pain and trauma. It can go very deep. It can become intense. I hope it happens. When it does happen, embrace it. Accept it. Do not judge it. It is a great sign. It means you no longer want to harbor pain within you. You want to break free from your prison of suffering. It is a sign of progress and change. It is a sign of wellbeing. It means you are growing! It means you are reaching higher. It means you are healing. Think of it as your yoga session that is putting you through some intense moves. It will be a powerful exercise to build flexible and beautiful body. It is an exercise towards your infinite potentials. It is a stretch towards perpetual honeymoon. When there is no pain, there is no gain.

You feel a shift happening. You feel you are ready to grow. You are ready to expand. You are ready to rise higher. You are ready to reach beyond the sky. You are sick and tired of being sick and tired. You are tired of living a dull, mediocre life. You know you came here to thrive. You are ready to turn your life into bliss. You are ready to transform from common to supernatural. You are ready to transform your whole life from ordinary to extraordinary.

You do not want to live in fear. You do not want the world to control you. You do not want to feel powerless or meaningless. You feel your unlimited energy broiling within you. You feel the atomic energy ready to be unleashed. You are ready to tap into the treasure within you. You are ready to make your life a beautiful dance. You are tired of hardship. You want to be flown to the tunes of your own dance. You are ready to live life of euphoric fairy tale. The greatest truth is that it is available for you. You do not have to travel anywhere to find it. It has always been within you. It is in the core of your existence. You have to decide to open the door in order to unlock the glorious prize within you. Truth will allow you to do that. Truth will let you step out of fear and beliefs that are not you.

Truth is not designed to please. It is not made to fit into any pre-manufactured, culturally acceptable boxes of proper values or beliefs of others. Things might appear out of the ordinary. It is only because you are leaving the ordinary to embark into the extraordinary life ahead of you. Things might shock you. Things might rock you. Things might even offend you because it is everything out of the norm of the preset morals we have been conditioned into believing. What you will find out is that there is no good, bad, right or wrong and that things just are until you start judging them.

Things are only a matter of a perception. It is a matter of how you look at things. You always have a choice how you view things, people and situations. That choice is a reflection of not only who you are but also who you truly wish to become. If you want to continue to stay the same, you will fear and hate. If you want to change and grow, you will love. Through love, you will find acceptance and compassion. Only love can open doors for growth. Only love can make you rise higher. Only love can allow you to connect with others. Only through love, you can see yourself in others. Only through seeing yourself in others you can truly feel and be compassionate. Through unconditional love, you will find the courage and the pressing need to expose the truth.

Time has come to awaken the brave You. The unlimited You. The fearless You. The You that is true to his or her true purpose and why you came here. This is your journey to return back to yourself. This journey is to arouse the truth within you that is same for all of us. This is not time of criticism or blame. This is not time for conflict and war. It is time to welcome honesty back to our lives. Honesty that will help you evolve into a kind human. Only honest truth will allow you to heal your life.

This is time to silence the mind and open the heart. This is time to sing and dance. This is time to celebrate life.

Painful Beginning

> "He who is not courageous enough to take
> risks will accomplish nothing in life."
>
> *-Muhammad Ali*

My very first entrance to this world was not easy. It was a very long delivery and painful labor. I was a large baby. I was breached. It became a life threatening situation for both my mom and I. The doctors had to act fast to protect both of our lives. The technology was not the greatest back then. We were running out of time.

I was being depleted of oxygen. I needed out fast. The doctor grabbed me by my right arm, which was the closest. He yanked me out. This completely dislocated my right arm out of the socket and damaged the nerves. I was blue and not breathing. They had to bring me back. It was a major trauma for both my mother and I. While I was alive the birthing experience did not leave me without a scar. The lack of oxygen created a great deficiency in my brain that would cause moments of panic and fear for no specific reason throughout my life. It took many years for me to point it back to this very first experience and realize the root cause of depression building up. So, there I was. A brand new baby, now handicap.

My right arm was nonfunctional and the neurologists informed my mother it could never heal. It was beyond repair. The damaged nerves can never be reinstated. I will be disabled for the rest of my life. It was the most devastating news any new mom could receive. My mother saw a brand new being she brought into this life experience to shine her light that was now handicapped. Her daughter will never be able to have a normal, happy life. She would be marked for life. She would be denied of all the incredible potential within her due to physical limitations. My mother could not accept this prediction. She knew her little girl deserves better and that she has to figure things out. She knew she has to develop a plan.

My mom came up with two options. The first option was that she must find a method how to beat all the odds and make a miracle happen. She had to make my arm mobile again. This meant to go and find a way even if it meant to travel to the Moon if she had to.

The second option was to create a life that would exceed my physical limitations. This would mean to surround me with an external world of the best. It would entail the finest education, the finest clothing, the finest of everything this world has to offer to build my confidence and strength that I would never feel of anything less. She knew very well from her own experience what it means to be an underprivileged child and how cruel the world can be. She did not want her little girl to ever feel the same.

She had to decide quick and put her actions into movement from the moment we came home from the hospital. She was thinking fast. It was not easy. This was time of no Internet, telephone, nor computers. Researching anything was intensive manual labor. It was nothing like today where at a press of a button anything you are searching for is presented right in front of your nose in a comfort of your living room.

Research back then meant trips to libraries, traveling to seek experts and spending endless hours of talking to people. Despite all the difficulties and obstacles, she decided for an option number one. She decided to make a miracle happen. She decided to give her precious daughter the life she deserves. She decided that her daughter's arm will heal. She decided that her daughter will not be handicap. She decided that her daughter will live a normal life.

My mom did not want anyone to tell her otherwise. Her inner intuition and faith was telling her that it can be done. Her higher intelligence exceeded any doubt of any medical men that were telling her otherwise. My mom knew. Once she made that decision, that commitment, there was nothing that could stop her. She had to unleash her supernatural.

My parents researched everything possible. It was tedious and exhausting work. They did not have to travel to the Moon though. They found it right here on this planet. Thank God. It was a method to induce external pain or shock. This pain would stimulate nerve synopsis into life protective mode leading into life-surviving motor activity. It was using brain functions into retraining the muscular movements.

Our nervous system creates programs that control our posture, movement and gait. This 'motor control' is primarily established during the first critical years of life. The method emphasized neurodevelopmental aspects of motor control in order to assess and restore dysfunction of the locomotor system and associated syndromes.

It was a drastic and mentally exhausting method for both of my parents. The therapy was invented by a neurologist who had to flee the country because of it. The method was made illegal. Some of the exercises were disturbing and extreme. For example, one of the exercises was for my parents holding their newborn baby by her feet and pretending they are pushing her off a table into the floor. The life survival reflex kicked in and a movement in my arm was being stimulated through a secondary nerve. Another exercise involved covering a table with a rough sand paper and having their baby crawl across it on her elbows. The sand paper induced physical pain. My elbows were bleeding into flesh. I was screaming from pain. It was heart breaking for my parents but they could not give in. There were similar exercises and they had to be repeated every two hours. It took an incredible strength and faith not to give up or give in. It took beyond-this-world dedication and determination. My parents were ridiculed and judged by others how can they be doing such things to their newborn baby. If it was today the social services would be called for sure and I would be removed for child endangerment.

My parents and I did this for the first two years of my life. That was our life. Every day, every weekend, every holiday. There was no time for breaks. There was no time to feel sorry. There was no time for any pity party. We were on a mission. We had only limited window of an opportunity to make my arm heal. It was the tough but unconditional love of my parents that inflected pain in order for me to heal and have a normal life. Anything else is just a 'monkey' love as my mother calls it. It is just being sweet, nice and 'loving' while doing nothing because we do not want the other person to feel pain. That kind of love does no good to anyone. I am the walking proof.

If it was not for the excruciating pain I would be handicap today. My right arm would never develop nor be active. It would be short lifeless limb attached to my body like some kind of trophy. I cannot even imagine in comparison to the strong physical form my body was able to develop into thanks to an unstoppable faith, physical pain and unconditional love of two amazing human beings. I am proud to call those people my mom and dad. I do not think that I can ever repay them nor return all that they have gifted me with.

What my parents did for me was not only on a physical level, however, it went much deeper than that. It went into my subconscious programming. The two years of living in a life survival mode evoked an inconceivable lust for life within me. It aroused thirst to fight and survive under any condition. My parents send me on a path of a warrior. Being a warrior has become the signature of my existence.

Wisdom

"More the knowledge lesser the ego, lesser the ego more the knowledge."

-*Albert Einstein*

Every baby born is a divine gift to this world. It is the gift that assures us that there is still hope and faith in the human race. Every baby that arrives is like an empty book for his chapters to be written. Every person is a beautiful book of amazing stories. All of us are authors and have so much to share. Every story is different and unique as we all have come here with one specific purpose. That purpose is to learn. We came to this life experience to feel, to smell, to touch, to hear and to see the incredible beauty that Mother Nature has created for us to admire. We all came here to learn. We all are just students of life. We are all just trying to figure things out. No one ever walked out of this life knowing it all.

The tree of knowledge is infinite. There is so much to discover and to know yet. Just the fact that ninety-seven percent of the ocean remains a mystery today is an amazing wonder. It might make you wonder what the depths of the ocean might reveal. It might make you wonder what kinds of creatures are living in there. It might make you wonder what these creatures, who have never seen the light of the day might look like. It might also make you wonder what the rest of the Universe hides from your eyes. It might make you wonder if we are the only beings here or if there are beings similar to us in a different galaxy, possibly somewhere out there. All of these scenarios are brilliantly mystifying and almost chilling. How little we truly know and we think we know it all!

There are three types of students in life:

- **Innocent student**

    The first type is the *innocent student.* He is the student that does not know and is not aware that he does not know. He is the simple student.

- **Foolish Student**

    The second type is the *foolish student.* He thinks he knows because he has studied a lot.

- **Blessed Student**

    The third and last student is the *blessed student.* He knows that he does not know. This is the reason why he is the blessed student.

We all come here as innocent students. We are eager to learn and study. We want to eat from the tree of knowledge although we have been warned not to do it. The blessed ones before us tried to advise us: *'You need nothing to be happy but the moment you learn, you need something to be unhappy about.'*

The moment you were born, you were amazed about the magic everywhere around you. Everything was fascinating and thrilling. You were fascinated by a bee collecting nectar. You were fascinated by a button on your father's coat. You were fascinated by the clouds in the sky. You were fascinated by the breeze moving through the leaves. The entire world looked like magic to you. Then you started to learn. You learned that the bee is just a bee. You learned that the button on your father's coat is just a button. You learned that the clouds in the sky are just clouds in the sky. You started to learn things, their names, and their labels. You learned that there is nothing more than that. You saw that everything is just a label and behind the label, there is no more wonder. The names and labels became barriers in the path of your wonder.

We want all children to eat from this tree of knowledge to become something, to become someone. We want our children to become sophisticated and complex. We want them to achieve a sophisticated level of foolishness. Some children make it only through high school. Some children make it through college. Some children pursue their degree in foolishness through a master's degree. Some children extend it to become lawyers, doctors and PhDs. All these beings become great 'ex-spurts' in something. Each 'ex-spurt' has expertise in something but knows nothing of his own brilliance.

We all want our children to know and for that reason, we send them to the finest schools possible. With that, their transition from innocent student to foolish student is inevitable. However, to evolve from the foolish to the blessed student status, something completely different must happen. You need wisdom for that. Wisdom can only be attained when you become suspicious and curious about your knowledge. It is when despite all your knowing, degrees and titles, you still want to explore all that is unknown and unexplored. You want to gain profound awareness through your own discoveries, through living yourself. You want to explore the wonders of the entire Universe on your own.

It is when the foolish student becomes tired of being just a trained monkey, repeating jumps in someone else's circus that the change happens. You simply get tired of mere schemes, models and concepts. You get tired of repeating the teachings and dogmas of others. You want to break free from all of that and dive into the unknown. It is right here in this moment that you unleash the revolutionary force you are and become truly creative. You become the blessed student.

Becoming a blessed student is a painful process because you will have to drop all the known things in your life. You will have to drop your ego. It is not going to be easy because the ego is going to fight you. It will fight anything and anyone that questions your knowing. It will take major courage and faith from your side. It will necessitate courage from you to make the jump. It will require a leap of faith. It does not mean that someone will magically erase all your knowledge; what it means is that you simply ascend it so it can no longer hold you down.

When this happens, you will cut your chains off. You will step out of the dogma of the known into the unknown. Not everyone will make this leap of faith. Those who decide to remain foolish students of life will fight with everything they have because blessed students are a threat to the system. They are independent thinkers. Blessed students do not conform. Blessed students can no longer be trained in anyone's circus. Blessed students appear dangerous to the foolish students. Foolish students and their massive establishment will do anything to destroy blessed scholars as they did with Socrates, Jesus, John Lennon or Martin Luther King, Jr..

Going beyond your knowing will allow you to understand that you do not know it at all. It will allow you to become the child of wonder and discovery again. A child that is fascinated with the majestic wonders of this Universe. A child that has a sparkle in his eyes and an unconditional love for life. A child that is fueled by his imagination that takes him beyond the skies. A child that is unstoppable. A child that is fierce and a child that is devoted to the unknown. It is exactly here where the magic happens. It is exactly here where inventions are made. And it is here where you can finally unleash the supernatural and evoke the genius within you.

Chapter 2

PURPOSE

"The two most important days in your life is when you are born and when you find out why."
- Mark Twain

Meaning of Life

Nothing in our life happens randomly. Everything happens for a specific reason. Nothing is an accident. Everything is created out of something. It is one of the founding principles of this Universe; it is the law of cause and effect. Everything is calculated and planned with the most meticulous precision. The fact that you are here, holds a great purpose and a deeper meaning to the entire life existence itself.

You are a crucial part of this entire ecosystem whether you believe it or not. Like every cell in your body is needed, the same goes for you on a greater scale of things in the Universe. You were not put on this planet to work from nine to five, send your children through college, spend money, and then die. Most people on their last day don't regret materialistic objects they did not get to buy. They regret not living a life of their dreams. At their deathbeds, they regret not appreciating the little things in life. They regret not doing the things they wanted to do. They wonder what kind of legacy or the lack of they are leaving behind. They regret being unable to experience something bigger and truly meaningful.

The truth is, we are all gifted but not everyone opens their package. Most people die without ever discovering the meaning of life and their purpose. They die with unfulfilled dreams and gloomy regrets. I am here to assure you that you have a big purpose as well. You are here to find your gift and then give it away. You are an expression of a magnificent light, yet to be discovered. You are literally a shining star and you are aware of this meaning deep inside. You are aware of this either consciously or unconsciously but you do know it. You might have caught a glimpse of this feeling. You are just not able to figure out what it is or where it comes from because you are unable to find the true self. The feeling you caught a glimpse of, it is a special higher calling, and it is the reason why you came here. If you are lucky, you might figure out what it is.

It took me forty-four years to do that. I had to return to love and my true self. It was done through accepting the truth and taking full responsibility of my life. I had to understand that I am a creator of the reality I wish to experience. My journey was one hell of a ride. It took me through a lot of suffering and pain that was both physical and mental. I was lost and confused. I was asleep. I was searching everywhere outside, but within. I had to keep looking into myself by going deep into the depths of my being. I had to keep looking for my love, my passion. I had to keep looking for my purpose in life.

To find yourself and your purpose, you have to search on the inside. You have to keep looking and go deep. You have to keep exploring yourself, instead of exploring anyone else. You have to look for the truth. You have to find your value. You have to get to know yourself. Only then, you will know what you need versus what your mind makes you believe you want. You need yourself to become your true self. You have to step out of the limited beliefs and social conditioning. You must decide to stop being a victim of life. You have to decide to reclaim your powers. You have to decide to unleash the supernatural within you.

You have to open your eyes to the sweet lies that you have been telling yourself. You have to dig out your true self that is buried underneath all those illusions and inner fears. You have to see the path of self-destruction you are on. You have to recognize the people around you, who are also feeding you sweet lies. You have to open your eyes to see the truth. You have to accept the truth and stop hiding from the reality. You have to transcend from all your fears. You have to confront them and allow yourself to heal.

You have to understand that situations and people who trigger you to feel negative emotions are divine messengers. They are couriers of the unhealed parts of your being. There are so many unhealed parts. Your whole body and entire existence is filled with pain. Your potential physical state of dis-ease is merely a reflection of your non-physical state of uneasiness.

I took everything personally for the most part of my life. I blamed others for my problems and misfortunes. I was driven by materialistic glitter and made my life all about me. It was all rooted in fear. While I was rich on the outside, I was poor on the inside. I was living in an endless lack. I never knew when it was enough. I was like a hamster in a wheel racing nowhere. I was racing with the herd that was headed in the wrong direction. I was just following the masses as we have been trained to.

Once I healed the physical and non-physical state of my being, everything shifted. It was the truth that set me free. Everything happening to me and my life started to make sense. Suddenly, like magic, it all came together like little pieces of puzzle. It all started to make perfect logic. Every single thing I have always questioned and could never figure out became clear. This was the biggest triumph and accomplishment I could have ever achieved. It was as if I was standing in front of a large audience, receiving an ovation.

For my entire life, I was sitting on the top of a treasure box without daring to look inside. I was a beggar with a fortune right underneath her nose asking others for a spare of a change. I was depending on others to be in charge of my happiness. It was up to the outer world if I was happy or sad. The outer world was in charge of how I was feeling on the inside. I was such a drifter.

When my endless search for everlasting bliss and happiness finally came to an end, it brought a startling inner peace and an unimaginable level of faith. I was complete. I was enough. I had enough. From there on, I could go live a life of purpose. It was no longer about me. My life became about the others.

False Self

> "You can either be a host to God, or a hostage to your ego. It's your call."
>
> -*Wayne Dyer*

My parents raised me to build the best character possible. Like most parents out there, it was crucial to create the most perfect image of their child for the entire world to see and admire. This was only because it was the way their parents raised them. Their parents followed the same pattern because that's how society functions. It has been done for generations in the same way. From early on, my life was centered on crafting the most flawless persona for the neighbors, teachers, friends and the rest of the world to adore. While this seemed normal, I was struggling to find any logic in it. To me, this always felt very unnatural because it was in contradiction with what my soul yearned for. My soul wanted to be itself with all the wonderful imperfections. Yet, I had to paint the most beautiful mask and put it over my real face every morning for the day. Once the mask was created and made up, I had to wear it at all times.

Hiding my true self did not feel right to me since a very young age. I felt like I could not breathe. In truth, all these maneuvers to project a perfect image gave me great anxiety. I could feel an inner battle broiling inside me. I found an outlet in rebellion. I knew I was born not to conform. I realized I was born a rebel. I was different and going with the herd was simply not for me. This is how I went about living my life. It turned me into a *difficult* child even though I tried hard not to cause any trouble. I only wanted to be me. I wanted to be accepted for who I am and not for who I *should* be.

I wanted to be happy. I wanted to observe the world and indulge in all the wondrous things around me. I did not want to worship someone else's ideals or ideas. I wanted to be true to myself and do what fits with my vibrations. I wanted to be in tune with my own harmony. I did not want to play someone else's song. They were all telling me to do everything but play my own tone. *"You need to be this way. You need to be that way."* It made no sense to my soul as it was out of harmony with my existence.

Before finding my true self, I had no idea what was going on. I had no idea that the outer world and all the people with their ideas about me, were programming my subconscious mind and separating me from my consciousness. It was a conditioning that was building a false self. This false self was my ego being built up. As a result, it would take me away from my soul and create a great deal of suffering.

"Know thyself." says Socrates. *"Know thyself."* says Buddha and many other great spiritual teachers. They are the ones who discovered the sacred message and purpose of existence. They are the awakened and the enlightened. Eventually, we all want to be like them. We want to learn the same ancient knowledge to find the eternal bliss. They want us to know *who we are* but we have no idea. We attach ourselves to our body and to the mind. The mind runs on ideas of others and the information that was given to us. It can be Christianity, Hinduism, Communism, Atheism or believing in unicorns. This makes you feel like you belong somewhere and it defines *who you are.* You say, *"I am American. I am Catholic."* and this becomes a feeling of knowing yourself. Now, you know *who you are* or so you think.

But, you are neither American nor Catholic. Your magnificent existence cannot be possibly contained by such a limited and primitive label. Your existence is infinite. Your being cannot be captured by such a trivial tag.

I knew that I do not want to be reduced to such a regulated label. I was everything but that defined label. I was a wild energy swirling within me without any specific order or ruling of the society. I did not want to be contained or owned. I did not want to become a slave to dogmas and beliefs of others. I did not want to control nor be controlled. I did not want to be regulated or reduced. I believed in speaking my truth. I had to tell the truth even if that meant standing alone. Telling the truth is never appreciated in a world of sweet lies. In fact, it is something I have been reprehended for my entire life. It turned into a never-ending inner battle for me to control what I can say and what I can do. I could never feel free to be myself. With years passing, I could feel the lack of true freedom growing bigger. I knew that one day; I will have to break free somehow.

Understanding Yourself

> "Knowing others is wisdom, knowing yourself is Enlightenment."
>
> -Lao Tzu

We, humans, pay so little attention to our thoughts, emotions, and feelings. We know we all have them, but do we truly understand them? Are we even in charge of them? Can you say that you are the boss who runs the business upstairs in your brain? Or, is it rather the people and the environment around you that is in charge? Perhaps it's your boss at work or your spouse at home that can make you feel happy in one moment and horrible in the next?

It is almost as if this phenomenon did not exist. It is almost as if we are some kind of pre-programmed robots on an assembly line. Our true thoughts, feelings, and emotions are not considered. They are only not considered but they are not even allowed because we have been programmed to conform to specific ideas of illusionary perfection. Yet, they are crucial energies carried throughout our entire system that translate into chemical and neurological functions.

These are the energies that set us into a state of ease or a state of disease. These energies are all we are. Without them, we would be lifeless machines moving around without any personal uniqueness. We would all be mundanely alike. We would all be boringly perfect according to our assembly line design. Despite the fact that the establishment invests many efforts to turn us into these machines, it will never succeed as long as humans can think, feel and produce emotions.

The issue on hand is that we do not understand who we truly are. Due to this, we find ourselves in a world filled with problems. In order to understand who we truly are, we need to de-clutter the problem. The solution to our world issues lies in the creator of the problem, hate, and tragic misunderstanding between human beings. The core of the problem is the individual. It is you and I. We are the trouble, not the world as we think of it. The world is an illusionary entity that is made of people like you and I. It is built on our relationship between each other. The world is only a mirror of who we are. It is a projection of our state of being. We have been very slow in understanding this. The wars we have engaged in and the millions people killed by its own kind in the last century alone shall demonstrate the great disconnect between us. We are like the cells in a human body fighting each other. It is what cancer is. It is when your cells no longer work together as one unity. This is where humanity is finding itself. We became one large cancer disease spreading on this planet. It is our belief that our doctor, president or the United Nations will solve this world problem. It is a wrong belief that the next leader will fix the problem for us but that day never comes.

Only you and I are the ones who can change the world by changing ourselves. You might think, *"Who I am? I do not have such powers! I am no one. I am too small."* right? You think you are no one. You think you cannot impact the world in such a way. You are too small to change the world at such a massive scale. If you think that, then you have not possibly spent a night with a mosquito in your room. If not, I would strongly recommend it. The little insect that is eight thousand times lighter than you will show you its powers. It will keep you up the entire night. It will make you search for it everywhere. It will make you run around like a maniac. It will tire you out and make you miserable. It will be on a mission and will not give up until it succeeds.

PURPOSE

It is crucial to understand that no matter how little your own world might appear, if you change yourself, you bring a new perspective. The new perspective is a different point of view to your everyday existence. By doing so, you affect the world around you. The people you affect will consequently affect others. Before you know it, there is an avalanche happening because it takes only that one small part getting loose to let the mass unleash.

No revolution is planned according to any set rules or standard. It all starts with knowing the Self. This self-knowledge is the gate to a wisdom and the beginning of a transformation. It is breaking the chains that are no longer serving you. It is breaking free from the fear-based beliefs of others that keep you weak. You think that you know the Self but that's exactly the problem, *you think*. It is the mind and the powerful subconscious programming that makes you believe you know everything.

To understand the self is the highest level of awareness and super consciousness. It is a state where the mind becomes quiet and tranquil. It is a state where there is freedom from any specific belief and dogma to any particular way of being or form. When you know that you are unique, you realize there is no special blueprint or pattern to follow your uniqueness. Only you can know once you unlearn all that you were forced to know. If you want to discover who you are, you need to stop having ideas or beliefs of who you should be of whom you are not.

If you are selfish, envious and greedy it is rather an art to become fully aware of that fact. This realization requires an extraordinary honesty and clarity with yourself. It requires full acceptance of reality and *'what is'* without a judgment. There must be absolute liberation from fear in order to understand and accept *'what is'*. This is extremely difficult because *'what is'* is never the same. It is not static. It is a fluid movement.

You are *what is* not what you wish to be. You are not a copy of some ideal because even the ideal is only an illusion.

If you want to truly understand someone, you cannot condemn that person. You cannot judge the book by its cover. You have to study and observe him or her. Not on a socially acceptable level but on the vulnerable, the dark, and the weird level. You must go deep and love the subject of your study unconditionally. If you wish to get to know your child, you need to love him or her as they are. You cannot judge them. You should play along with their imaginary stories. You need to observe their thinking and submerge yourself into their inner world. You cannot judge or condemn them. You have to try to put yourself in their shoes. That is the only way to truly get to know them.

To truly understand anything entails an alert mind. While it entails an alert mind, it also requires a passive mind that is free from judgment. It is a mind where everything just is. The absolute knowledge about the Self does not come from your knowledge, your title or degree. It does not even come from an accumulation of experiences, which is hardly a memory cultivating. When you know yourself, you become very creative because you are unleashing the genius within.

You become true uniqueness and it reflects on the things you produce, which might be art, starting a new business or making the next greatest invention. Most people are hardly creative. They are like a record, playing the same song repeatedly. Their song is the same melody based on the collected knowledge of others put together in a different order, sprinkled with special effects. It is, however, still the same song copied. It is because we are constantly searching for methods and ideals to worship, which murders the true spirit of creativity.

To understand yourself is a matter of seeing the true self in a mirror and how you relate to everything there is. It is your relationship to property, not only yours but the property of others as well. It is your relationship to not only 'your' children but also the children of others. It is your relationship to the environment around you. It is your relationship with the planet and the entire Universe. It is your highest conscious relation to everything and every being around you. This is a state of highest alertness and super consciousness, which comes only when you tend to be your true self. This is the death of ego and the false self. While it is the death of the ego, it is the birth to your true Self. It is the You that you have been searching for everywhere and in every experience.

This transformation will transform the world. This is the only transformation that can end our wars, disease, unemployment, hunger, and class division. Before the world can transform, we must transform. The transformation begins within yourself. It is not according to some ideology or belief because that would be only conformity to a specific format. It is the revolution of the Self. This is the only solution to our problems.

CHAPTER 3

MOST IMPORTANT WEALTH

"The doctor of the future will no longer treat the human frame with drugs, but rather cure and prevent disease with nutrition."

-Thomas Edison

Climbing the Corporate Ladder

I arrived to America with ten dollars and a green suitcase. I knew no one. I hardly spoke English. I was no one. I had nothing. Despite *my nothingness*, I was full of dreams and great vision. I knew what I wanted and where I was headed. I made it to the land of opportunity, and all I had to do was to roll up my sleeves and get to work. I was going to live the American dream into its fullest extent. There was not a single cell in my body that had any doubts.

It was a cumbersome journey with a lot of obstacles. It was only a few weeks into my new residency when I had a head on collision in a borrowed car. I was uninsured and could not afford any medical help. The only thing I had was my faith that I will be ok and so I was. I had no higher education nor money to go to college so I learned on my own. I had no computer nor money to buy it so I built one. I had no connections nor network so I started at the very button and slowly climbed the ladder.

"I will become a Vice President, travel the world, and make a lot of money one day," I would proudly tell my family and friends. They were all skeptical because I was no one. It was impossible with no background or training in the field. It was only a matter of time for me, though. This was how I saw life and its opportunities. The opportunities were limitless. I could already see myself where I wanted to be. It was not just a dream.

I was aligning myself with a frequency of that destiny. I was tuning into the harmonic tone of my vision. My vision became me and I became my vision. There was not a single cell in my body that did not believe in the destiny I had decided for myself. As far as I was concerned, it was a done deal. Now, all I had to do was to get to work.

I carried myself as if I owned the world. This was the way I was since I was little kid. It was that early on survival mode of warrior that got instilled in me. It was programmed into my DNA through my hardship and pain. I was destined to conquer and triumph. Failure was not an option. The sense of survival was deeply planted within me. It was stamped into my existence. I started as a secretary and worked myself into a vice president position within a few short years in a high tech field dominated by men. I traveled the world in first class. I ate caviar at five star restaurants. I drove around Italy with executives in Ferraris. Life was amazing. I was on top of the game. I was living the American dream.

Deep inside, however, this same drive and hunger for more success, for a higher status and more money was disconnecting me from my true self. I felt as if I was becoming more of a machine and less of a human being. I did not know exactly how to process it. I did not know how to make sense of it. I started to feel confused and lost. I was not aware of what was happening. I thought it was a normal process of maturing to have level of uncertainty, stress, and anxiety. I put it aside and kept going. I kept running a race. Where I was racing to I had no clue.

Race to Nowhere

> "Have no fear of perfection,
> you will never reach it."
> -*Salvador Dali*

I wanted more and more. I was competing everywhere and with everyone. I wanted to be the best. I wanted to be the smartest. I wanted to be the most admired. I wanted to be the most successful. I wanted to be at the top of the very top. No matter how hard I worked and no matter how much I achieved, there was always someone higher than me to compete and compare myself with. I started to sleep less and have major anxiety.

Having butterflies in my stomach became my normal state. There was no peace within me. I was living in chronic stress. It was my mind controlling what I should be. I was never enough. While I was a wealthy executive and picture of the perfect American dream story, I was no one on the inside. I became an empty shell. The condition was building up to dangerously high stress levels. Over a period of fifteen years, I climbed the corporate ladder. I was gaining recognition, titles and building prestigious image to become someone.

My ego loved it. It couldn't get any better than this. My hunger for material things became bigger. My needs became larger. My world's biggest worry was when American Airlines stopped serving caviar on their first class flights. I reached the Platinum level with the airlines for one million miles traveled. I felt very proud of myself because I had what others wanted to have so badly. *"Here you go, you've spent one million miles up in the air away from your children doing what? What is the purpose, really? What did you accomplish for others, this planet and your life?"* was the voice in the back of my head questioning.

It was the inner voice. It was the inner whisper inside my head I could not turn off. I worked long, stressful hours so that I could buy a bigger house in a prestigious neighborhood. It did not take too long and I bought several houses. I was buying and buying. I wanted more things than any one person would ever need in a lifetime. I was sucked into the corporate treadmill that I soon realized was taking me nowhere. There was an immediate thrill and gratification but when that feeling wore off I came to the realization that I really had nothing. I had no real purpose. I had no real direction. I was just drifting through life. I could no longer feel myself. I was just decorating myself and my life with fancy things. I was a body performing different duties and playing different roles. I became a puppet of some kind of imaginary show.

I was on top of the world living the American dream. From nothing I succeeded to have everything: beautiful family, diamond rings, expensive cars and luxury homes. Yet, I still felt completely empty and unsatisfied. Was this it? Is this what we live for? To make the situation worse my health was at its ultimate worst. I gained weight. I was taking multiple prescriptions. I was on antibiotics every other month. I had surgeries, therapies, and doctor appointments, all in an attempt to cure my diseases. I was seeing many experts for many different parts of my body. No one could tell me where the pain and sickness was coming from. No one could tell me what is going on. There were no answers or logic. There were only mysterious diagnosis and more drugs prescribed. Sickness became inseparable part of my life. Nothing made sense anymore.

I grew to accept that being sick was just simply going to be a part of my life. If I had a few days in between it felt like a major triumph. It felt so victorious and wonderful to be healthy. I did not want that feeling to end. Looking back at it today, it is shocking how quickly we become acclimated to new conditions. When a little pain starts all you can do is focus on it but as time goes on, it slowly becomes part of who you are. You simply accept the fact that your lower back hurts, that you have digestive issues or that you have high blood pressure. It is almost like one forgets how it feels to be really healthy and energetic.

I became the sickness expert. From all of my personal experiences, I knew everything about colds, infections, fibromyalgia, migraines, digestive issues, candida and many other health issues. I knew all the medications and was in constant search of what additional drug could heal me or what new expert to seek. My body was falling apart. It was trying to speak to me through all the different discomforts. The issue was that I could not understand its language. I put my health into the hands of others. I trusted that they knew better and had my best interest in their mind. What I missed to see was that as any other industry the medical world is also for profit. Selling drugs, cutting organs and keeping me powerless was the way to make money on me. I missed to understand that I need to seek doctors only in times of emergency. It is for urgent care until the body can pick up its own healing process. Healing is always and exclusively a biological process. It is never chemical or mechanical. Healing is only performed by what created the body in the first place. My life was falling apart. I was stretched to the maximum. My stress level was in its ultimate high.

Stress is a very important natural function that protects us from dangerous situations but the issue is that we have adopted stress as part of our lifestyle. We turned ourselves into chronic stress machines. Chronic stress became twenty-four seven affair day after day. The problem with that is that our body can only function in two states - growth or protection. When we are in the growth mode, everything works, as it should. Millions of cells are replaced. Existing cells are nourished. We prosper. We heal. We thrive. However, when we are in the protective mode, all the functions are seized by the stress hormones. It reminds me of the stories my grandma used to tell me during her times of World World II.

During the war when the sirens would go off, it meant instant alarm to stop whatever everyone was doing and run for a bunker. The bakery shop would stop making the bread, the butcher would stop preparing the meat, the schools would close and the factory would shut down. The entire city would stop producing, close things down and run for protection. Then the threat would be over and all activities would resume.

But what if the sirens went off for a very long time? How long could you actually survive in that bunker? Maybe for a few days? Maybe for a month? It would all depend on how many supplies you brought with you to the bunker. No matter how well you would have planned, you could not survive for an indefinite period. Eventually, you would run out of water to drink and food to eat. Your body would start to suffer from the lack of nourishment. This is exactly what happens when there is chronic stress and unfortunately it is the current state of affairs for most people. They are literally hiding crippled in a bunker.

The stress just does not stop. There is the economy to worry about, the terrorists, the war on cancer, the issues at work, the problems with your kids' school, the concern for your aging parents, your siblings, and all the million remaining issues of our chaotic world. When you are in the stress mode the release of cortisol and adrenalin does not stop. Your body no longer grows. It remains stuck in the limited protection mode. Only your legs and arms are receiving available oxygen and nutrients through the blood supply. It shuts your immune system and you become highly susceptible to disease. Your body performs this process so that you can run away from the bear chasing you. Once you outrun the bear, you go back to your peaceful state. There is a great difference between real danger and illusionary fear.

Fear can be anything our mind imagines, which is usually not a real danger. There is no bear chasing us. It is projecting the possibilities of dangers – things that usually do not happen ninety-nine percent of the time. Danger is real. It is when you are alone in a dark alley and someone is trying to kill you. Or you have just experienced a car accident and need to get out of danger as other cars are approaching. This is real danger when the body needs to partially shut down in order to focus all your energy to get you out of the dangerous situation. In that moment when you are being chased by a murderer, you do not need to grow new cells. You do not need to digest your food. You do not need to support any other growth mode physiological functions. Your body's primary focus is to run out of the danger. When you live in chronic stress you cannot run away from it. You are constantly being chased and literally killing yourself.

Delusion of Becoming

"Man – a being in search of meaning."
-Plato

You want to be happy. You want to experience forever bliss. What is happiness? What is bliss? Is it a status to achieve? Is it a destination to arrive at? It is something that you have to become.

You have been made believed that happiness is somewhere on the outside. You have been tricked that bliss is somewhere out there. You have been deceived into a destination addiction. You have been lured into a hamster wheel that the system keeps spinning faster and faster on you. It wants you racing. It does not want you to ever realize when you have enough.

Happiness is a state of being. Becoming is a pain and anguish. Becoming is a misery. Becoming is depression. It is a separation between ego, your false self, and your true self. It is a separation between the roles you have been conditioned into and your soul. You became your mind and separated yourself from your heart. Even when you say *"I feel happy"* you are not really happy. You think you are happy and that is your problem. It is your mind making you believe and for that you can be happy in one moment and sad in another. Every feeling you have has to pass through your thinking process that will decide. For that you do not have control over your feelings, as it is ruled by the mind and its subconscious programming.

Take for example writing. There is a difference between an author and a writer. A writer has the knowledge on how to write. He knows how to put words together and deliver the news. He works through his head. It is his mind at work. He is a writing expert. He writes but he is not absorbed by it. Author, on the other hand, gets lost for hours in his passion. He writes novel, science fiction, or non-fiction. He gets completely absorbed by it. He wakes up at three o'clock in the morning and writes nonstop. He loses concept of time. It is just him and his art. He is an artist producing an art. He is. He is not doing. He is not performing a duty of any kind. He is not performing a job of any kind. He is no more. His thinking has dissolved into this heart. He is just a passionate flow expressing itself.

When you find your passion, you get completely absorbed by it. You are excited. You are blissful. You live in a state of fulfillment. You are in a state of euphoria, and for that, there are no boundaries. You are no longer doing. You are no longer becoming. You are being. It is only when you are not fully connected with what you are doing, the job you are performing, you are miserable. There is a resistance and the results reflect on your state. That is why most of all you do is mediocre. Your job, your relationship, and your life. You are constantly becoming and performing something. You are not being.

Euphoria is the highest level of excitement. Euphoria is wild. Euphoria cannot be controlled. You are beyond yourself. You are completely immersed in it. You experience ultimate bliss. Only wild people can afford euphoria. The ordinary man is too smart. He is calculating. He is analyzing. He cannot afford euphoria because euphoria cannot be controlled. Euphoria is only for the crazy and wild who let go of fear-based mind.

When you are genuinely happy, there is no ego. Have you noticed? When you are truly happy, you have lost sense of the self and immerse into what is. You are the moment. You are all there is. There is no mind. There is no time. You feel deeply connected with all there is.

Euphoria is the ultimate liberation. The crazy truth is that you do need not travel anywhere to find it. You already have it. It is in your very own existence. All you need is to make a decision that you want it. You have to decide you want to unleash the supernatural.

Disease Delusion

> "The art of medicine consists in amusing the patient while nature cures the disease."
>
> *-Voltaire*

I had to travel on a business trip to Korea. I had been traveling there for years. It meant many hours on the plane, days full of meetings, followed by late nights of drinking and socializing. It was exhausting. It was during this trip that I finally hit my breaking point. I became extremely sick while I was there. I knew that I couldn't live like that anymore. It was there where I was introduced to the idea of detox. *"Detox? I am not an alcoholic. I do not think that this is really for me,"* I thought to myself filled with judgment. I was very desperate to find a solution, though, since nothing coming out of the medical community made any sense to me.

I had nothing to lose at that point. I started to read and research about detox, body cleansing and holistic approach to healing. This pivotal moment set me on a journey of discovery. A journey of tremendous struggle, very low moments, doubt, and misery ended up leading me to an incredible light. I would have never been able to see it if I had not confronted the darkness within me.

It was after this trip I discovered two lumps in my groin and armpits area. I was already dealing with sporadic fevers, digestive issues, night sweats, and being tired all the time. Finding the swollen lymph nodes was only a confirmation that my cancer was real. It was no longer an intuition I could feel. I manufactured lymphoma in my body. My heart dropped and I could feel it beating in my stomach. I spent the entire night crying myself to sleep. I could not get my mind off the discovery.

While my mind acted surprised, my soul knew about it all along. It was now several months since my birthmark above my right eye had started to grow as well. I knew that I had been growing cancer in my body for years now. I had to confront the reality and stop pretending. It was one of the scariest moments I had to face. There was no more hiding from the truth. There was no more pretending that someone would come to save me. There was no more time for false hopes of magical pill to cure me. I had to pick myself and become my own hero.

I was on a downward spiral. I knew that I would only have a short time to live if I didn't make some dramatic changes in my life. I could see my life disappearing right in front of my eyes. I was scared. I was having excruciating yeast infections that were not healing. My body was infested with candida. I was out of energy. I felt exhausted all the time. My body was slowly shutting down one disease at a time. I lost the lust for life. Everything started to look gray. It was not only my body but also my spirit giving up as the disease was sucking the life out of me.

I was only thirty-eight. I saw my life slowly disappearing in front of my eyes. I found myself not caring anymore because of how exhausted I was. I had no one to turn to. I could no longer trust the medical industry. It was as if everyone was poisoned with the same belief. I felt as if no one could see what I was seeing. I felt that no one could understand what the medical experts were actually doing. No one could see the great disconnect.

No one could see that the medical industry was not about helping people heal but was about making money like any other business. I hit the lowest of the low points. I was alone, by myself, with only my failing body to keep me company. I felt betrayed. I knew that I could not turn to the same people. I had no trust and it was my survival instinct telling me to run away. It was only my doctor mother who knew what was going on. She wanted me to get tested but I refused. I knew what the results would reveal. I realized I can go nowhere close to a hospital. I knew that if I did, I would not come out alive. I knew that once they get me into their system they will threaten me with death if I do not follow their poisonous treatments. That was the last thing my body and my mind needed. I knew that I was too weak and in the most vulnerable position to fight off such a pressure and force of people who cared less. I could almost see the future unfolding as it came all clear only a few years later when the system almost got me with my gallbladder emergency. This was way more serious situation than just one organ. I had to be smart. It was a point where I knew I must take charge of my own health.

I realized that I am the only one who knows her body the best. No one else could ever know my body better than I did. It was my strong natural instinct that was protecting me. I had to listen to it. It was the voice of God within me guiding me. It was the Universe caring for me. It was so strong. It was so powerful. I could no longer defy it. My ego, on the other hand, did not want to accept the inconvenient truth. It was in denial of my own wrongdoing. It was looking for someone or something else to put the blame on. Maybe it was something in my genes. For sure it had to be something there. Or maybe there was some incorrect mutation that had happened down the road when the genes were passed over to me. My ego did not want to take the responsibility that it was actually me who built the disease.

My ego couldn't accept that this had happened because I had ignored all the signs my body had been sending me for many years. The years of colds. The years of infections. The digestive issues. The weight gain. The fatigue. The fibromyalgia. The migraines. The candida. All those were caused by years of eating white bread, pastas, crackers, pretzels, cheeses, deli meats and everything in between. The years of chronic stress and living in fear. All of this had led to the inflammatory messages my body tried to communicate to me. My symptoms and diagnosis was the language in which my body was speaking to me. I am sure it would give me a phone call or send me an email if it could but it cannot do that. It can only speak through discomfort and pain to awaken you in order to take action towards healing.

I was too busy building and chasing my career as I was made to believe to make something of myself. Here I was, an accomplished Vice President of a high tech company being respected by my peers, my family, and my community while I completely lost a respect for myself. I lived life of luxury. I had it all yet the most important thing was no longer there in my life. At that moment, I realized that health is truly our most important asset and the only wealth.

What do you really have if you lose your body? You cannot do too many things without your body. Actually, you cannot do anything without your body. Can you finally see?

I recognized I have been asleep for most of my life. I was brainwashed and pacified into accepting the wrong beliefs. It was time to face my own lies and wake up. I had to acknowledge that it was me and only me who went so far to build cancer in her own body. It was no one else but me who was too busy to take care of the most precious thing I will ever own. I was blinded. I had to take full responsibility. I had to start taking care of myself. I had to face the consequences. I had to fix things right away before it was too late. It was also in that moment I realized how loving my body had been to me for all those years. It was taking care of me. It was giving me life. It was loving me and it was time I started to love my body back.

It was time to pay back and start taking care of myself. It was not the cancer as some vicious act of evil. It was me who created chaos in my body through the stress, the Starbucks fancy coffee drinks, cheese, steaks, white bread sandwiches and lack of sleep, just to mention a few. It was my cancerous lifestyle. I was out of touch with life. I took my body out of balance and ease. I put it into a state of dis-ease. My body was trying to compensate and love me for a long time but eventually, it ran out of resources. I was selfish. I was not loving myself. I was only taking and taking, and never giving back.

Anytime I would get sick I would make the situation even worse by drugging my body through antibiotics and medications. I did that since it was what everyone was doing. It was a quick and easy fix. I did not take the necessary time to heal properly. I was always on the go. Being sick was inconvenient for the life that I lived. I never really removed the root cause of any of my issues and it started to accumulate. I did not understand the circumstances. My body could no longer take the abuse. It had to respond to the situation. There were not enough nutrients or oxygen in my body to support the healthy functioning of my cells. I had unconsciously poisoned my own body setting and caused a mutation of my cells into carcinogenic cells.

My body was giving me a last chance through lymphoma. My cells had to look for an alternative energy supply and they found it in sugar. There was plenty of that in my toxic body and that's what they claimed as their natural progression in the crisis. They could have just dropped dead but they were too loving. They wanted to make me live till the last resource. My cells were hoping I would be able to get the message and improve the situation. It was then that I realized what cancer truly was. It was not an enemy but just a remedial process to preserve the body as long as it can. It was my own ignorance and loss of true values due to which I could not see the good through the bad.

Cancer is a loving process. It happens to possibly give us one last chance to wake up and see through our own wrongdoing. Despite how scared I was, I felt blessed. I knew that this was not how I was going to end. I had too much to live for.

> "Everything has beauty but
> not everyone can see."
> -*Confucius*

Born Warrior

> "The successful warrior is the
> average man, with laser-like focus."
> -*Bruce Lee*

My life was never easy because I was born a warrior. Warriors cannot have it easy. They must be tough and resilient to deal with any kind of situations that life brings. That is what makes life exciting and worth living. Life of bliss is not for the weak. I knew this is not how my story will end. I had so much to live for. I had so much to give. I had so much to discover. I knew I had to survive and start searching for the real answers. I knew that I can no longer trust the medical community with my health situation. It was a shocking discovery but the real truth. I had to open my eyes and accept it.

    I needed answers to my medical issues and I needed them sooner than later. I had to do my own research. My intuition, my inner voice knew that I was designed to be healthy. I knew that I will heal. This began my exploration and education of the wonders of the human body and the healing powers of the Universe.

My higher intelligence was telling me to stop focusing on my diseases like the medical world has taught us to do. Instead, I focused on finding the root cause of all my suffering. I needed to stop looking at the end result and go back to the beginning, where everything had started from. It is like when there is a pint hole of water leaking in the attic. You do not immediately see the leak. It is small but it drips little by little until it accumulates enough of water to start making its mark. You do not see where it is coming from, but you do see the wall in the living room bubbling and the carpet building mold from the water. When you see it, you do not go to call a specialist to give diagnosis. You don't call them to tell you that your wall is suffering with walletitis, inflammation of the wall in plain English. You don't call them to tell you your carpet is suffering from carpetitis, inflammation of the carpet. You would not let them prescribe some mysterious chemical to go over the sick, damaged walls and on top of the old, moldy carpet. That would be insane. You would call these experts fraud.

What you do is, you immediately go to look for the root cause. Where is the leak coming from? Once you find the leak you stop it first. Only then you can start repairing the damages. You scrape the damaged paint down. You rip the moldy carpet out. You let everything dry out. You let everything heal. You do any necessary repairs first and only after that, you install new carpet and put a new fresh paint on. Doing anything else would not only not remove the actual root cause but it would make things much worse. Your body works no different. I did not wake up having a cancer from a mosquito bite. I did not contract it from a friend of mine. I manufactured the disease myself through my stressful, mindless lifestyle. It was also me who had to get to the root cause of it to heal for good.

Medical experts study specific diseases and learn on dead bodies. They get so mystified by the disease that they lose focus on what this is eventually about. The goal is not to understand disease but to understand health. Where does cancer come from? This is something you have to always ask. Anyone who is advertising such cure expertise must be able to explain it in plain language that a child can understand it. If he does not know how to explain it nor where the disease is coming from how can he cure the condition?

Cancer is a result of years of toxic accumulation. When toxins accumulate in the system and are not removed, it leads to tissue irritation. This puts tissue on a fire. It is called inflammation. If this inflammation persists, it develops into chronic inflammatory issues and will manifest itself in the weakest area or organ. Inflammation has names such as vasculitis, gastritis, hepatitis, pancreatitis, meningitis, dermatitis, arthritis and many others.

If this is not resolved, the existing toxins literally eat at the tissue and create a void which is called ulceration. As a result, the tissue hardens and the body needs to address the existing toxins somehow. It encapsulates them. This is called a tumor. A tumor is nothing more than a bunch of trash build up which has not been taken out for years. At this point, the body is out of balance. Several of its functions are affected. Healthy cells no longer have the needed oxygen nor nutrients. There is a state of toxemia in the body. Normal cells mutate and no longer need oxygen to function. Now they just feed on sugar. They function on their own. They create an abnormal situation in the system.

A German doctor Otto Warburg received a Nobel Prize for his work in the area in 1931 demonstrating how normal cells turn carcinogenic. He was not the only one. There have been many other doctors confirming the same. The reason you will never hear about them or their findings is that cancer is a big multi-billion dollar business. There is no business in finding a cure and please do not be fooled when they make you believe otherwise. There has been over three trillion dollars invested in cancer research since the war on cancer was launched in 1971. Just follow the money and find for yourself if you have any doubts. Knowledge is power. In this age of information being so easily available, an ignorance is a choice not an excuse.

I realized I was looking for my answers in the wrong places and with the wrong people. It felt like one big theater. My medical experts appeared in roles of bankruptcy experts. All they knew was to diagnose a problem and bring me closer to my health bankruptcy. I realized they are not the ones to build my health, my most important wealth. I needed different type of knowledge, different type of experts. People who actually care about others and me. Honest beings that are not there just for money and profits. This was deadly approach. There is no money in healthy and dead people, but there is a lot of money in sick people. It was a crude awakening to what's really happening around me.

I buried myself in studies of toxicology, nutritional science, physiology and a science of life. The more I read, the more light shined on my situation. Things started to make sense. It was all coming together. The diagnoses were that I was toxic! My body was dirty inside. I needed to clean up the house. I had been overmedicated for so many years that my body could no longer function properly, let alone heal itself. I was literally falling apart. I had finally found the answer I was looking for. Through my extensive research, trial and error, and intense determination, I finally succeeded in developing a healthy, natural, and simple way to detox my body.

Everyone thought how risky it was what I want to do. They were all doubtful. I knew better. My inner voice was speaking louder than anyone else. There was no other way. I knew what I had to do. I knew I was onto something big. I could just feel it. I went towards it at the full speed. I was excited. I knew deep inside I am going to solve this overdue mystery of mine. The most difficult part was to convince my ego driven mind. It was so used to listening to others. It was used running in the old program within its comfort zone - within the known.

It is very hard to go outside of your own box. It is, however, outside that comfort zone where you find yourself and where life truly happens. It is when you embrace the uncertainty and unknown because you are sick and tired living mediocre life. It is the inner knowing that you are distant for great things and for that you have to step out of the old. In that very moment you realize that when nothing is certain anything is possible.

Winners Never Quit

> "You will face many defeats in life but never let yourself be defeated."
>
> *-Maya Angelou*

The first few days of my detox protocol were hard. I was extremely nauseous with flu like symptoms. It is a completely normal reaction to toxins leaving the body. Most people do not realize and assume it is the detox making them sick while the detox is igniting a release of the bad stuff from the body not the other way around. I knew there was a beautiful healthy energetic body inside of me somewhere. I had to find my strength. I could not give up. I painted a picture of a healthy and energetic me. I programmed it into my mind. I would feed my mind with the new program. The body had to simply follow the new set of instructions.

I detoxed diligently for three weeks. It was an incredible start. Every day I was seeing and feeling changes in my body. Some days were easier than the others, but overall I could feel myself getting healthier day by day. It was encouraging. I knew that this will change my life. It was the best feeling in the world! When I finished my three weeks of cleansing, there was literally a brand new person in me that was born. I could not believe my eyes, what miracle three short weeks can do. How such a short period of time can undo years of wrong doing. It only proved to me how forgiving and loving our body is.

My skin had cleared up. My infections healed. I no longer had digestive issues. My fibromyalgia was non-existent. My candida and my migraines were gone. I could not believe how simple it was. If I had only discovered this years earlier. In the process, I lost twenty five pounds and my love handles I struggled with for years. I had more clarity in my thinking. I was glowing. I was no longer living in my "sick bubble". It was a true transformation. I continued on cleansing my body for several months to ensure any of my cancer cells are gone out of my body. I knew that I beat my cancer and that I will never again give it a chance to live it in my body again. It was the most liberating feeling ever. I won and I had the recipe to continue winning.

Great Deception

> "It is always much easier to task to educate the uneducated people than to re-educate the mis-educated."
>
> *-Dr. Herbert M. Shelton*

As I was detoxifying and healing my own body I also started to feel a shift in my mind. I was starting to have an incredible energy and mind clarity like never before. It was clear to me that I was not only purging toxins from my body but was also removing toxins from my brain. I started to see things for what they truly are. For example, I would watch TV and hear a commercial for a drug. It showed happy people talking how a specific drug is healing their arthritis. Then the commercial would go on to talk about the horrific side effects such as numbness, chest pain, new joint pain, hives, vision problems, infection, lymphoma or even sudden death. This was delivered in the same happy, pleasing voice like it was perfectly fine to exchange joint swelling for sudden death. I could not believe what I was hearing. I wondered if anyone else was hearing the same. It seemed that no one else did. I wondered how is it possible for our society to approve a drug that could cause such harm?

As I was opening my eyes and removing the layers of our society conditioning, it was like peeling an onion. You remove one layer and surprise! There is another! It was one surprise after another until I realized this is a part of the great plan. I came to understand that the society is not broken but it was designed like that. It was all about money no matter what the cost.

To program conditioned citizens into a fear based, disease laden, medicated robots who can no longer think for themselves. System that feeds on its people as its source of life energy. System that turned its citizens into money-milking cows. From selling drugs that were completely legal, meat packed with antibiotics, girl scout cookies filled with heart disease causing poisons, drinking water poisoned with brain-damaging chemicals to energy drinks filled with cancer-causing toxins. And if the human kind was not enough the system also targeted our beloved pets with the same agenda to make us even more suffer when we see our beloved four-legged best friend dying of cancer and other diseases.

An article in The Washington Post in 2016 was one of the many that warned the public about medical errors that are now third leading cause of death in United States. Medical errors claim over two hundred thousand lives every year more than car accidents or stroke. It is seven hundred people killed per day that is absolutely not necessary. It is a shooting of an entire neighborhood or three commercial airplanes crashing killing everyone on board per day. I am sure that this kind of news might catch an attention of a few!

"It boils down to people dying from the care that they receive rather than the disease for which they are seeking care for," said Martin Makary, a professor of surgery at the Johns Hopkins University School of Medicine according to the article. Professor Makary leads the research and confirms that this category includes anything from bad doctors, wrong diagnoses to communication breakdowns.

Human existence on this planet dates to over three hundred thousand years ago. It was not until the mid-nineteenth century that the first synthetic drug was introduced. It was chloral hydrate in 1869 that gave rise of pharmaceutical chemistry and medical profession, as we know it today. Yet, man somehow succeeded to live and thrive all the hundreds of thousands years prior to pharmaceutical drugs, oncologists, or heart surgeons. The evidence is in his success to spread over most areas of this planet. He populated the Earth from the desert, mountains to tropics and to ice lands.

The way our ancestors did it was by following the laws of nature as all other animals continue to do so in the wild till today. These animals are true to their roots and for that, they do not know what diabetes, heart disease nor what cancer is. These beings live in a harmony with the founding laws of life and for that, they live joyous life of abundance. They eat only real food, drink water only, get their sunshine and fresh air. They do not lock themselves in artificial buildings filled with chemicals, stale air, and no sunlight. They do not spend their free time shopping in malls or watching worthless things on TV. They do not rush through their existence like there is somewhere else to be than in this life. Animals are unlike the 'intelligent' human stressing his life away and building disease.

Majority of the human intellect is spent on researching and developing poisons to treat the sick. It brings a fundamental question: "What a sane mind would want to administer poison to a person that is already sick?" Wouldn't you wish to do exactly the opposite? Wouldn't you wish to restore the sick's man state of ease and remove the root cause of dis-ease?

No matter how much we are trying there is a huge disconnect in the medical and pharmaceutical world. The history of medicine is a major fiasco. The results of the medical industry are not only uncertain, unsatisfactory but also very misleading to the gullible public that was made to believe their lifestyle has absolutely no connection to their disease. It made the unsuspecting public believe that health is for the medical experts to deliver through poisoning and cutting organs out.

When you examine the deeper truth, you will find out that what we call a progress in medicine is in most parts disregarding drugs that were once sworn by and replacing them with new drugs. The way your medical doctor is ready to discard, the old drug and the way he embraces a new drug should teach you one very important lesson. That lesson is that everything is simply an experiment until there is a new trick on the market that will deliver a new hope and new promise of a magic cure. That day, however, never arrives. You have been brainwashed into medical fallacy where your medical experts can no longer think straight.

The true purpose of pharmacologists is to determine how much of poisons can be given without causing an immediate death. How much can the generic body handle without producing great harm that would be immediately visible. This kind of approach is destructive. It is not for-life nor to restore health. It is to manage disease and build more disease in the organic system. *"It is simply a plan of poisoning the sick on the implied assumption that if the poison does not kill it cures,"* writes Dr. Herbert M. Shelton in a book called The Myths of Medicine that every medical student and person who wishes to enter the healing world should read. It is for anyone who wishes to make sense of today's healthcare crisis. Dr. Shelton's extensive work in health restoring research is recommended for anyone who wishes to thrive instead of to suffer through life.

"These men (medical doctors) plan way of doubling their incomes and come to the public with the plea that they are sincerely interested in the health and welfare of our children and that they put over their income-increasing programs for the health of our babies and for the welfare of the school children. They are as cold-blooded as any class of criminals on the whole earth. Indeed, I know no other class of criminals who live by crippling, maiming and killing babies and children," writes Dr. Shelton.

The medical establishment created a criminal monopoly built on deception and corruption. It is a master plan once you get to fully understand it. The medical experts name your discomfort in couple ancient languages and now they call it science. Disease is fascinating. It is fascinating what the body can create, and the variations when it is not in a state of ease. It is a disguise that captivated all the ex-spurts. Prescriptions are prescribed in a code language that no one but the physician and druggist can decode. The medical colleges fully support this injustice on human kind. The fact that the professors in these institutions continue to teach these fallacies is a tragic truth that is responsible for deaths of children and innocent beings as a result. Instead of teaching honest science and truth they are accomplice in the greatest deception of our times.

Realizing the raw truth sent me into a very dark place. I was angry and outraged. I felt alone and betrayed. I felt insulted. I felt disgusted. I was seriously disappointed at the world. I was infuriated with those in charge we trust the most allowing such an injustice on its own kind. While I healed myself on a physical level, I got ill morally and emotionally. I was going through a very difficult time accepting what is going on with our civilization and how others are being deceived.

Life turned negative: it was painful and very dismal. I could only see the problems and how doomed we are as species. It didn't matter what I did, nothing could make me happy. It was so hard and I felt like I didn't want to live anymore. Everything seemed so meaningless and pointless. I've entered a great darkness. I have entered a tunnel. Little did I know that I have entered a state of metamorphosis. I was transforming from a caterpillar into a butterfly. My wings were ready. I was a little clumsy caterpillar that has eaten enough from the tree of knowledge to get onto a journey into a completely different dimension. My horizontal journey was coming to an end. I was embarking on a journey towards the skies. I was about to rise higher. I was about to go vertically.

It was in this time of darkness that I got pulled by some mysterious force into studies of quantum physics and neuroscience. I needed to explore beyond the physical world and our limited senses. My soul knew there is so much more to discover. I had to immerse into an exploration of the invisible yet so powerful world of the infinite force of this Universe. I embarked onto the hero's journey.

Chapter 4

FREEDOM

"The only way to deal with an unfree world is to become so absolutely free that your very existence is an act of rebellion."

-Albert Camus

Freedom is your natural state of being. It is our very first birthright. The moment you left your mother's womb, you became free. Free to live the life of your dreams. You became your own free agent. You became your own being and freedom is your absolute state. Why is it though that you do not feel quite free? Why do you feel all kinds of pressures? Why is it that you feel stress and anxiety? Why is there a feeling of a voice in the back of your head that is telling you something different?

You know exactly what you want. You precisely know the life you want to live. You know where you are headed and the things you want to accomplish. Yet, somehow, you are unable to quite get there. It is as if everyone got it figured out, except you. There is a nagging voice in the back of your head, which is second-guessing all your decisions. This voice has all kinds of concerns. It wonders if you are good enough or correct. It wonders if you can do it or if you are deserving. The voice urges you to hurry because you might die soon. This voice is like a dark shadow looming over your big dreams and amazing visions. It does not think that you can do it because it is afraid. The voice is afraid because there is so much to fear.

Many things can go wrong and you might fail. People might laugh at you or they might even dislike you. Failing might make you lose money. You feel that your spouse might leave. Failing might make you homeless. You fear that your children might hate you. There are so many things that can go wrong but most of all, you fear that you might end up all alone. You're afraid you will die and no one will even notice.

You are afraid of pain and suffering. It is both physical and nervous pain. You do not want disease because that brings physical pain. To prevent that from happening, you surround yourself with the best doctors and specialists to ensure your optimal health. They run all kinds of tests to ensure you are in the best shape possible.

Despite the results showing you are well, you are not free of the nervous pain. You worry because of the history of disease in your family. You worry about the cancer your mom died from and the high blood pressure from your father's site leading into a heart attack. You worry about the diabetes your grandparents suffered. You worry about the horrifying disease statistics. You cannot rest. You keep looking for anything that could go wrong. You keep asking the medical experts to run additional tests.

When they are unable to identify a problem, you seek out other experts because you think there must be something wrong. You seek a holistic doctor to stop this pain. You take marijuana to numb your suffering. You become a detective assigned to the strangest case of unresolved mystery. Looking for a disease becomes your mission. You will not rest until you find a lead, something that can take you to this mischief. You are unable to relax until you find something wrong. You need some type of diagnosis that can finally put your medical team to work and you to rest.

FREEDOM

The psychological pain is fear of losing the things that give you satisfaction and pleasure. You love to feel satisfied and pleased. Being celebrated, popular and the center of attention are all things that you love dearly. You love to be needed. You need the assurance of others that you're worthy. You are afraid to lose what delivers those feelings of gratification and respect. You fear to lose it all. You fear to lose what you cherish so much in life.

You are afraid of losing your wife and family. You fear losing your job that provides for the lifestyle you have. This lifestyle provides your loved ones with a good life so that they can love you. The job and money are tools to keep you nicely decorated so you can keep attracting people. Money and status is your honeycomb. Your job and lifestyle provides for your love. You need that love to function. You know deep down within you that you need the energy of love, which is the source of life. Love makes who you are and why you are. Without that love, you would suffocate. You know that without love, you would die and you are afraid to die. You fear that without the job and with no money, no one will love you. The source of love supply will be terminated without a job and money. You will be cut out of your life support. You fear of feeling worthless and ending up all alone. This entire idea horrifies you.

Many things can go wrong. In fact, almost anything can go wrong. Nothing is guaranteed in life. So, you need to ensure you took every precaution for safety. What do you do? You purchase as many insurance policies as you can. You install the latest security systems in your house that can be monitored from your phone anywhere you go. You surround yourself with the best experts. You have financial advisers, the best doctors, and the best of all in each profession available.

Despite the fact that you have the best of all you can think of you are still unable to completely dissolve the inner fear of something going wrong. The reason is that anything can go wrong at any given time because life provides no guarantees. The only true guarantee in life is that you are here right now and one day you will not. Life becomes fear itself, which takes over your existence. Fear will want you to feel nicely tucked in, exactly where you are, in the same spot you have always been. It wants you to stay in that comfort zone which prevents you from venturing out of the safety zone. This comfort zone prevents you from reaching the sky because you fear of falling down.

What happened to all those dreams and aspirations you once had? What happened to the brave heart and romance for life? People happened to you. The moment you left your mother's womb, everyone got together and started to program you with their subjective perception of the world. Your parents, siblings, uncle, aunt, teacher, priest, and idols gathered to instruct you who you should become. They programmed you with the things you shall or shall not be. At this very moment, where the programming of your subconscious mind started, the program gets reinforced every day. This programming is not yours, it does not resonate with the energy of who you are. This is where your inner conflicts starts to take you from a state of ease into unease. It is a state run by fear.

Where fear exists, there cannot be freedom. Where there is fear, there cannot be love. Love is the opposite of fear. Therefore, you cannot be in a state of love and the state of fear at the same time. Either it is one or the other, you can fear or you can love. There is nothing in between. When you love, you will know because you feel amazing. You have a feeling of honor, respect, and self-worth. Love creates a sense of belonging, acceptance, and certainty. You have a feeling of abundance. You have a feeling of being fully satisfied and fulfilled. Love makes you feel happy. There is a bliss and joy. You radiate because when you love, your body fills up with the most powerful force. There is no other feeling other than love. You are at peace.

On the other hand, fear has many diverse masquerades. Some people will say that they do not have fear, but little do they know that fear can be disguised. Fear goes undetected by the mind because the mind is fueled by it. Fear feeds the ego so it will naturally avoid disclosing its own life source. Fear represents itself as pride. It appears as hate. Fear shows up as anguish. It acts as doubt, it performs as sorrow, or it pretends as desire. Fear appears as anger. Even being neutral comes from fear.

There are numerous different ways how fear can make its debut. The only way you can identify fear is by knowing that neither of those feelings feel good in your gut. The way you can tell is that you are searching. You have desires and needs. Your gut knows about these needs. It is a connection to your inner wisdom. It is your higher intelligence and you can never escape its review. It is always there watching over you.

You became enslaved by the mind. Your feelings and emotions are in control and you can never shut them off. The whole world lives in psychological prison. Our entire world is suffering from psychosis. Our thoughts, feelings, and emotions are so impaired that we lost contact with truth and reality. How has this happened? Where did we, as humanity, took such a wrong turn? We got lost on our journey. We have been raising our children to become slaves. We became slaves of social, political and belief ideologies. We have not taught our children to think on their own. We have not taught them to be true to who they really are. We have not taught our children how to become their own person and cultivate that divinity within them.

In order to heal from the psychosis that is spreading like a black plague, the world requires a new way of raising our children. We need to empower our children's individuality. They must be allowed to grow to be more intelligent, more independent, more conscious, and more alert beings. This cannot be achieved through any sort of belief system. It can only be achieved by giving them a permission and incentive to search for the truth. It will require them to be encouraged and reminded to seek out their own honesty, their own findings that will liberate and set them free. Nothing else can do it, only the truth can set us free.

Near Death Experience

> "The day science begins to study non-physical phenomena, it will make more progress in one decade than in all the previous centuries of its existence."
>
> *-Nikola Tesla*

It was Wednesday and I went for a business lunch meeting. I ordered a salad and an ice tea. I enjoyed the meal and the meeting went very good as well. Later in the afternoon, I started to experience a stomach discomfort. I was not paying too much attention to it. I thought that it might be just something I ate at the restaurant since it was not food I prepared myself. I was drinking plenty of water and went about my business for the rest of the day. I started to feel the same discomfort but much intensified at dinnertime. *"I must have food poisoning,"* I thought to myself. *"There had to be something in my salad,"* I reasoned. The pain was getting worse and worse. I end up on a floor of our living room in excruciating pain. The pain was awful and felt like giving a birth. It was as if thirty bones were crushed at the same time. I knew that I had to get through it and so I did.

The next morning I put myself on an intense detox to kill the bad bug I must have contracted. I did it for several days. I was ready to resume eating my regular, healthy, solid food on seventh day. The moment I ate solid food, the same agonizing pain came back and along came the same attack. I was rolling on a floor crying. These attack episodes lasted for about six hours and I had about eight of them.

After my ninth episode, I was rushed to the emergency room. They performed an ultrasound and revealed I was suffering with a large gallstone lodged in my bile duct. It blocked a bile flow and created quite the disaster. That is why I was in such a severe pain. I was diagnosed with acute cholecystitis, acute hepatitis, choledocholithiasis, infection, and gallstone. I was devastated to hear the news. After all I have been through, I was thought of as an image of health. I was crushed.

I had best team of doctors. They performed MRI and told me that my gallbladder is severely damaged. The walls were inflamed and hardened. There was ulceration and it was beyond repair. My situation was urgent. I was close to going septic. I spent the entire night in the hospital crying in disbelief. I spent the night soul searching and asking questions. Why me? Why now?

During that night, I had one more attack. The pain at this point became unbearable. Of course, I was not taking any pain medications because they were not going to heal me. It would be only to mask the issue and there was no need for that. The pain was like giving a birth three folds. It was excruciating. My whole body was shaking. My entire body was filled with so much pain. It was agonizing feeling. I could feel every single cell in my body screaming. The pain was piercing throughout my entire system. It was tormenting. Seconds felt like days. It was beyond any imagination. I have no idea how many hours the pain lasted. This episode was the most painful and I could no longer hold it.

There was nowhere else to go. I had to surrender. I had to let go. I had to let go of all I cherished. I had to release. I had to surrender to what I feared the most. I had to accept what I could not change. I had to let go of all I loved. This was it. I had to leave my life behind. I had to say goodbye to my entire family; my parents, my husband, my loved ones and my two amazing children. Saying goodbye to my beautiful sons was the hardest part. I could see the tears in their eyes. I could see the huge void in their lives. I didn't want to go. I was horrified. I was scared. I could not believe that this was it. I was only forty-four years young. I felt like I was only a baby. I was just getting started on this life experience. I have been already through so much suffering.

There was no other place to go, however. There was no other escape, there was no other salvation. I had to go. I had to accept that the end is coming. There was so much sorrow and pain but there was no other way. My eyes closed and I entered darkness. It was like being locked in a large cave that did not have an end. It was pinch dark. There was nothing there. There was no air. There was no sound. It was the most hollow emptiness I have ever experienced. It was cold. There was no one there.

It was just the most uninviting nothing and me. I realized I am experiencing death. At that moment, my mind stopped racing. I stopped fearing. I had to accept what was happening. I became calm. I turned into my inner self. It was the only thing I could do. I had to forgive myself for anything I might have done wrong that lead me to this point. I became peaceful and accepting of the situation. I turned into my heart to find the needed comfort.

Once I connected with my heart the most angelic light entered my space. It burst through a magic window. It was so bright. It was warm. It was loving. It was pure energy entering my entire body. It was the most liberating, orgasmic experience ever. It was intense. It was euphoric. I was filled with the most affectionate unconditional love. I have never experienced anything like that before. I could feel how I became connected to the source of creation and became that very light myself. I was finally free of all the pain and suffering.

My light dispersed everywhere. I was no longer burdened by any physical limitations whatsoever. I was finally free. I became everything and everything became me. I could now go anywhere I wanted in the entire Universe. There were no restrictions. There were no borders. There were no limitations. There were no conditions. It was just freedom in its most pure and divine existence. I traveled across the Earth and reached across the whole Universe. I could feel I returned back home. I could feel my wholeness and completeness within me. I was filled with peace and divine bliss.

I felt complete and fulfilled. Through the shining light, there was a message for me. It was not spoken or written. It was a vibration that told me I have to return back. It told me I have to go back to heal my organ. It told me that I have seven days to do that. I did as I was told. I came back and told my doctors what I am planning to do. They all thought that I am crazy. They thought that I lost my mind. *"You have no idea what you are doing,"* my primary surgeon told me. *"You are in a critical condition and will die if we do not remove your gallbladder,"* he continued.

"And if you don't die you will be rushed back for a major surgery where we will have to slice you open across your entire abdomen area," he finished in an aggravated and annoyed voice. He called couple more gastrointestinal specialists and surgeons to make me finally surrender to their outnumbered powers. They were all hovering over me like scavengers over a pending feast. I was scared. I was horrified. I felt bullied to the highest extend.

The pressure of the medical doctors was tremendous. They were pushing the risk of potential poisoning, pancreatitis and most importantly the threat of death. My family only brought an additional pressure. They all wanted me to follow the advice of the experts. I was on live chat with my mom as well to hear her medical opinion. She was no different from the rest. They made it all sound so easy. *"Gallbladder removal is a fairly simple surgery,"* explained my doctor. *"We do them all the time. You will be completely fine,"* he was trying to assure me. *"Hmm, that's interesting, doctor"* was my reply. *"How do you know that I will be fine?"* I continued. *"You know what, why don't you come with me. Let's cut your gallbladder too!"* I answered. My doctor did not like that idea.

Imagine your body as a baseball team. You take one player out and the whole team is greatly affected. They might be able to carry on the game but the team will be handicapped. Removing an organ is the same no matter how 'unimportant' anyone tries to make it. It was designed through a divine purpose and removing anything is never a smart idea.

Gallbladder is no different. It is a bile reservoir. It absorbs water and makes bile stronger and better. Gallbladder is part of one of the most important functions of re-building the body every day. The process is called metabolism. Without it one of the most critical functions would be affected. Yet, the doctors made it sound like it is not a big deal. When I told my doctor at the hospital, what I am planning to do and why, he admitted that he is ignorant and not trained on the healing way of things. He just knows how to diagnose, prescribe meds, and cut organs out. It only confirmed the major disconnect. A disconnect that costs human lives.

The idea alone of someone reaching into my body, my holy temple, with their dirty hands to cut something that was there on purpose was simply against my spiritual belief. I could not envision it. There was no way. I had to go by the special message that was in a complete alignment with my heart, my inner instinct, and my higher intelligence. I knew that my body is designed to self-heal and self-repair. I knew that I can do it. I knew that my body knows the best.

I was in the hospital only couple of days but it felt like ages. It felt like a prison in there. There was no fresh air. There was no sunshine. There was no real food. There was no life. I could only smell death. All the people there were pale and overweight. Everyone around was sick. It was no place for me to be. I had to get out as fastest as I could. I had them to remove the gallbladder stone and then called my girlfriend to come to get me out of there. I ran as fast as I could from the hospital. I remember when I got out and could smell the fresh air for the first time. It was amazing. I looked up and I saw the most beautiful crystal blue sky. Birds were singing. The sunshine was feeding me its warmth. There were flowers and trees. They were all there for me. I was back home. I could feel an intense healing energy and health. I knew that I will be fine because I am loved.

Healing Miracle

"Be realistic, plan for a miracle."

-*Osho*

I came home from the hospital and created an intense seven-day healing detox for myself. I have added a few additional components specifically addressing the organ's inflammation and infection in my body. It was not only what I was doing as far as nutrition is concerned but also the non-physical and meta-physical aspect of healing. It was literally a healing trans I have immersed myself into.

I took a break from work and my entire life. I put my entire life on hold. It was all about me and healing myself for the following seven days. Even though I was physically in my house with my family, I was spiritually not really there. I still cooked family meals and helped out but only in a very limited way. I completely removed myself from the busy, stressful life running a company, dealing with family business and having kids to take care of. It had to become all about me. I had to become selfish. I had to become selfless. It was now or never. I had to beat all the odds. I had to heal in order to continue to be there for others. I had to heal my body because I needed my body to thrive in life. I knew that if I don't heal it would be much worse scenario. This was it.

What was seven days on a large scale of things anyway? It was nothing. It was hardly a miniscule sacrifice for great things to come. I had to do it and I had to believe that I can. This was all I had to do. I had to give myself the permission. I had to give myself the powers. I pretty much ordered my system to heal despite the tremendous discouragement and threat from the studied doctors telling me it is impossible. *"Who are they to tell me, anyway?"* I said to myself. It was no longer about who is going to allow me but who is going to stop me. I was on a mission.

Once I gave myself the permission, I made an agreement with the seventy trillion cells in my body. I literally spoke to every and single one of them. I clarified that we are a team and that we must pull through this together. I told my body that we must unite and that we need to heal the organ, which makes our world complete. Without the gallbladder, we are nothing. They all understood and from that day on we went to work. For the following seven days I got incredibly busy. I had a big world to run. It was the world of me and its trillions of residents that make my existence. I had to take care of them. I had to feed them only the highest healing energy possible.

I added a vibrational therapy, juicing, meditation, grounding, enema, immunity boosting and much more to my healing detox protocol. The healing protocol was to bring the body from a state of dis-ease back into a state of ease. I had to establish a health-affirming inner peace. I had to remove the disease causing stressors and establish equilibrium. I had to bring my body from a state of threat into a state of growth and healing. It was an intense protocol but I was worth it.

Through all I was doing, I was tapping into the infinite healing energy of the Universe, our life's source. The Universe was so loving and caring. I was being nourished like a baby and there was such an unlimited abundance available to me. I was astonished that I have never known this secret before. How come I have never been told about this? How could I have lived in such a darkness surrounded by people who know only darkness? Experts who only look for darkness while we have such an amazing healing power available to us right in front of us. I could not believe. I realized we are living in a dark age of ignorance and foolishness.

Within short couple of days, I started to see great improvements. I was feeling amazing. I have not been eating solid food for two weeks and yet had an amazing energy. I was on a healing high to best describe it. I could feel incredible energy rushing through every cell of my body. I had an incredible mind clarity. I was alert and in complete mindfulness. It was a heavenly feeling. I could feel how hard my entire body was working for my overall health. I could feel how the entire world of me was giving it all it got. It was an incredible collaboration of pure love. I was scrubbing all foreign toxins out of my body and carrying them out. I was bringing new nourishment. I was repairing every affected area in my entire body. I was rebuilding every damaged cell one at a time. I was streaming the most powerful healing energy into the damaged and sickened parts of my body. It was such a beautiful and smooth collaboration of all of us working together. It was astonishing. It was divine.

It was mind blowing to see the debris being removed after days of no eating. It was a gummy like fatty content resembling the intestines. It was cholesterol, fats and toxic junk stuck to the intestine walls that had to be removed in order to heal. I have lived a very healthy clean lifestyle for the past six years and detoxed religiously but there was still more to cleanse. It was residue from the years of my prior neglect.

Just imagine what might be hiding inside of you if you haven't detoxed recently? It was staggering to witness it. I went for a checkup with my naturopathic doctor and all looked great. He absolutely blessed my decision and wished he did the same when he was young and had his gallbladder removed. I knew my gallbladder was healing and that it will eventual function perfectly again.

I completed my seven-day healing therapy and went back to a normal life as if nothing happened. I knew I am healed. I knew it down to every cell in my body. It was everyone around me looking at me with a great suspicion. They did not believe that I could be possibly healed due to the life threatening diagnoses only a few days prior. I didn't mind their concerns but eventually the pressure became bit much because my entire family worried. I agreed to have a new ultrasound done. *"I hope it goes well for you today,"* everyone worried for me on the day of my procedure. *"Of course it will,"* I assured them. I wanted to have the paper finally in my hands. It was not really for me because I knew what the results will reveal. It was for my family and loved ones to give them peace of mind that I am fully recovered.

A week later the results came in. I went to my doctor and he said, *"I cannot explain this but looking at the ultrasound before and after it looks like two completely different patients. The new ultrasound does not show even a slight sign that anything ever happened to your organ. There is not even a trace of a damage of any sort!"* I smiled. *"It is a miracle!"* my doctor exclaimed. *"Of course it is! It is a miracle only because medicine cannot explain it. Our bodies are designed to do this every day, when we allow them to do their healing job and stop interfering."* I smiled back at him and we embraced in a long loving hug. I was officially healed and my loved ones could relax. It was official!

I healed a life threatening condition in short few days only because I made a connection with my higher intelligence that gives me life every day. It is an intelligence that operates my inner world and my entire existence. It consists of seventy trillion cell inhabitants that create thousands of chemical reactions every moment of my life. Imagine that power. Imagine that influence. I connected to the healing powers of the Universe. We came together and made an agreement that we are going to fix the problem. We made a precise plan. There was not a single cell in my body that had a doubt that it might not work.

This is how miracles happen. They are actually not miracles at all. It is what our body is designed to do once we tune in and listen. They are only called miracles or spontaneous healing because the mainstream medical field is not trained in this matter and does not understand.

Recipe for Miracles

> "Natural forces within us are
> the true healers of disease."
>
> *-Hippocrates*

There is a new field of study called psychoneuroimmunology that demonstrates the connection between the mind and the body. This new field studies the effects of stress on the immune system. The studies range from psoriasis, cancer to coronary artery disease and many other chronic health issues. Many of these studies are focused around cytokines as the body when in physical and psychological stress, releases them. Cytokines are small proteins released by the cells in the immune system. There are many different types but the ones stimulated by stress result in inflammation. They are consequently called pro-inflammatory cytokines.

Your body is designed to release pro-inflammatory cytokines as a response to an injury or infection to help destroy germs and repair tissue under normal conditions. However, when you are physically or emotionally stressed your body also releases certain hormones including epinephrine. These hormones then connect to specific receptors that signal for the production of pro-inflammatory cytokines. Your every thought produces a biochemical reaction in the brain. It activates the brain to release chemical signals throughout the body that act as messengers resulting in the way we feel. For example, when your eyes see and perceive something as a pleasure the brain instantly produces a chemical neurotransmitter called dopamine. This turns the body onto an anticipation of a pleasant experience and you feel excited because of it.

On the other hand, when you have negative thoughts such as perceiving things in anger, hateful or self-denouncing attitude such as *"I cannot do this. It is impossible to happen."* the brain now produces neuropeptides that makes you feel hateful, angry, and unworthy.

The problem is that our subconscious programming is very powerful and makes up for ninety five percent of all of our brain activity. Because our society has been designed as world of threat and fear, we have adopted the same mentality. We have been trained and conditioned to see the world outside of our inner circle as a threat. We do not trust, we worry and fear. We have been trained to be on constant watch out.

Unconsciously, we have been programmed into a state of war with everything. War has become our social state of existence. We constantly have to protect ourselves from the one million of things that could go wrong or attack us. We have been trained to be in a relentless fear. This results in majority of our thoughts to be negative. The more we think the same negative thoughts that produce the same chemicals that keep making the body to have the same feelings, the more we become modified by our thoughts on physical level. What we think we become. Our thoughts and the energy or intensity of these thoughts directly dictate our health, the choice we make and ultimately the quality of life we have.

Most people spent their life in an internal state of fear. This manifest itself as anxiety, worry, anger, grief, jealousy, sadness, envy, pride, doubt and many other forms of emotional pain. One's attitudes form a state of being that is directly connected to the physical body. For that, a person who wants to change their state of health has to change their thinking patterns. In order to do this one has to literally upgrade their subconscious programming. It is a special program that creates new synopses for neurons firing and wiring. You are literally upgrading your brain programming from a state of dis-ease and misfortune to a state of ease, health, and prosperity. Once you do that, you transform your life in profound ways beyond anyone's beliefs. This is the world of miracles I would like to invite you in.

Your body always knows and wants only the best for you. You just have to be able to tune in and align with the results you wish to achieve. The reason why this is a great mystery to the medical world is because they are taught to operate only in material world through means of drugging, burning, or cutting organs out. They completely omit the fact that each organ in our body is made of molecules that are made out of atoms, which is pure vibrational energy. This knowing carries a tremendous power and hope for true healing. This healing has no side effects but only benefits.

The truth is that your highest intelligence, the divinity within you, designed you perfect. It designed you to thrive and be healthy. You can feel this knowledge deep within you. I am not telling you anything new. I am not any more special in performing healing miracles than you. You have the same healing powers. Each and every organ in your body plays an important role and is there for a reason. Trust your gut feeling, your inner intuition. Do your own research and always follow the money. To remove my gallbladder would have been additional twenty thousand dollars for the hospital. That is a large sum of money and a great business. As for me, it would have marked me for the rest of my life. There is no money in this world that can build a new organ in my body. My organs are priceless. I would never be the same. I would be handicapped again and I had no interest in doing that.

The System

> "Government is not the solution to the problem. Government is the problem."
>
> *-Ronald Reagan*

Wisdom is not something you can go to study. It is not something you can purchase nor borrow from someone. There is no professor or guru who can teach you wisdom either. You cannot learn it from TV, books or Internet. To be wise, you have to sharpen your own intelligence. You have to become brave and courageous to immerse yourself into the unknown. You will have to look for the truth. You will have to embark on a journey of a path that has not been traveled ever before. You might have to go against the stream and against the crowd. You might have to stand alone because your discovery will be mind-blowing and it will be hard to accept by the mediocre mind. The truth will threaten the mediocre mind that is afraid to venture out of the box of limited beliefs.

The deeper you go, the more you will discover. The more you discover, the more you will want to discover. You will understand how much more there is yet to discover. Your search for truth will take you on an endless journey of unlimited potentials. The deeper you go, the more profound findings you will encounter. They will be earth-shattering discoveries. You will shake the grounds and right there, in those depths, the light will go on. It will hit you straight in the head and you will realize you have unleashed a genius within you.

"Let me tell you why you are here. You are here because you know something. What you know, you can't explain but you feel it. You felt it your entire life. That there is something wrong with the world. You don't know

what it is but it's there. Like a splinter in your mind driving you mad. It is this feeling that has brought you to me. Do you know what I am talking about?" Morpheus asks Neo in the movie The Matrix. The sci-fi movie from 1999 captured the attention of a lot of people. You were possibly one of them.

The Matrix is an intellectual maze with mysterious plot and fascinating dialogue to spark interest of the attentive mind. The movie raised many interesting questions and it left a lot of people questioning. Even more people did not quite grasp the message the movie was trying to deliver.

The movie shows us what might happen if we do not awaken to our higher intelligence and let the mind take over. In the movie, the main character Neo feels that there is something wrong with the world around him. Things do not fit the facts. Things do no feel right or natural. You learn that it is no longer the present but the future. It is two hundred years later, the twenty first century, where artificial intelligence has taken over the world.

The movie takes you into the future where the world we know has been destroyed in a war between mankind and machines. These machines were originally built by humans who could not foresee the future danger of artificial intelligence. These machines are kept in dark and no longer need sunlight as a source of energy. They took over the world and enslaved humans to farm them as a bioelectrical energy source.

The humans are kept in unconscious state and plugged into a central computer unit. They are there to feed the unit their bioelectrical energy. The whole world around them is programmed and nothing is real. Everything they experience and feel is just a virtual construct. The whole society around them is a part of virtual reality called the Matrix. Their brains are stimulated and controlled by a computer program.

This program makes them believe they are living a regular life in the twentieth century. They go to work, they eat, they sleep and interact with each other as if nothing is happening. They have been brainwashed and deceived about their true purpose and their existence.

A few people escaped the Matrix and know the truth. One of these people is Morpheus. He hacks into the Matrix and tells Neo, *"The world you see is the world that has been pulled over your eyes to blind you from the truth. Like everyone else, you were born into bondage, born into a prison that you cannot smell or touch. It is a prison of your mind. The Matrix is everywhere. It is all around us. Even now in this very room. You can see it when you look out of your window or turn your television on. You can feel it when you go to work. When you go to church. When you pay your taxes. It is the world that has been pulled over your eyes to blind you from the truth."* he continues. *"Unfortunately, no one can be told what the Matrix is. You have to see it for yourself."*

Morpheus offers Neo two pills and tells him to make a choice, *"You take the blue pill, the story ends, you wake up in your bed and believe whatever you want to believe. Take the red pill and you stay in wonderland, and I show you how deep the rabbit hole goes."* Neo is unsure, he takes a moment before making a decision. *"Remember, all I am offering is the truth, nothing more."* Morpheus says. Neo reaches out, picks the red pill, and puts it carefully into his mouth while reaching out for a glass of water. *"Follow me."* says Morpheus.

People who watched the movie and understood the plot will tell you that the movie is not really a sci-fi. The movie Matrix is actually a documentary. It is a documentary about where humanity is essentially headed if we do not awaken to what is going on with our world. It is trying to show us that our system is not broken but that it was designed to work in this specific way. It was designed to test our intelligence. It was designed to see when mankind will finally figure its erroneous way of living as species. It is for us to see that the matrix is our own society. It is our own world of exploitation that was created by ourselves. It is our establishment, into which we all feed through our own personal mental enslavement. It is all done through the generational programming into our self-limiting dogmas and beliefs that you need someone to govern over you. It is a belief that you are a powerless no one, who cannot sustain life on his own. It is a belief that builds you into a great agent of dependency. It makes you believe that you need some higher governing agency to give you permission to thrive in life. It is a belief that you need a permission to be happy. It is a belief that you need permission to be successful. It is a belief that you need someone to keep you safe. It is a belief you need permission to life. Nothing more erroneous can be further from the truth. It is time for us to realize that it is not some illusionary entity or agency, which got us into the global chaos where we find ourselves.

Let me give you a small taste of what is happening right underneath your nose in this moment. Only a hundred and twenty-five years ago you did not have to ask the U.S. government to go fishing or hunting. You did not need permission to collect rainwater. You did not need permission to own, build, or renovate your home. You did not need permission to start business. You did not need permission to get married either. Today, you need permission to protest, sell product or grow food on your own property. Little by little, you are allowing the matrix to chip more and more at your freedom. We have arrived to a time where you can practically do nothing without being extorted by the government and receiving their permission to almost every single move you make. If you believe you are a free citizen you are fooling yourself. You live in a tax farm as a free range human.

It is time to realize that no one other than you and I make our own society. We are designing our own problems through the choices we make every day. It is the disconnected way of living among us that results in the corrupted existence of our species. Our illusions are the life source for the establishment. We are its life energy because it cannot function without you and I. The establishment is very much aware it is the minority, which is why it invests a lot of efforts to keep you weak. It fears the day we wake up from the hypnosis we have been programmed into. It fears the day when we'll realize we are the majority. We are a *sleeping* force that will eventually wake up one day.

That time has come, you can feel the shift. You can see that things are no longer working. You can feel it down in your bones. It is time to awaken that sleeping giant and unleash the supernatural powers within you. It is time to realize you are your own free agent. You don't need anyone's permission. It is time to wake up to the realization that it is not some magical outer force that will come to save the world. The power and protection you seek lies within you. It is your inner power and transformation that carries the much-needed change.

Chapter 5

FAMILY

"Nature does not hurry, yet everything is accomplished."

-Lao Tzu

Infertility

I could not get pregnant. Every time we conceived, I kept having one miscarriage after another. I had over five miscarriages. Eventually, I stopped counting after the first two. It was too much to handle emotionally. It was awful and painful, mentally as well as physically. It made me feel like a failure. It made me feel as unworthy being. I spent days crying my eyes out. I felt useless. I felt I was being punished for something I did not understand. I could not make sense out of our situation. My husband and I were both young and healthy. Well, it was what our mind made us believe. Not having a disease diagnosis does not constitute health. Despite the fact that neither of us had any diagnoses, our bodies were not healthy. I did not know but my body knew better.

My body was unhealthy and toxic. It was too dangerous to carry a new life. My body knew better than my limited mind and my medical experts around me. We usually do not understand – or rather try to ignore – the signs that our body is always sending us. We are too busy with our lives for health related matters. We look to the educated men in white coats because we think they know our body better than the body itself. The truth is, however, your body and its own intelligence knows the best. Your body's ability to heal is greater than what anyone permits you to believe.

I had no idea that my body was smarter than me. My inner voice knew but I was afraid to trust it fully without medical advice. Through the miscarriages, it was actually trying to tell me that it was in a dangerous state and not in optimal health. I was too blinded to see it that way, however.

Instead of trying to understand, we always try to force nature. We are unwilling to stop and listen. Try to identify why the body is possibly rejecting pregnancy. You just want what you want. That is the end to it. It is also the established ambition of the medical field to control and dominate nature. To win over where the Universe works in complete collaboration. There is no fight nor is there a competition for the survival of the fittest, as the old Darwinian theory made us all believe.

I was no different. I was determined to have a baby. I started to see fertility specialist. They ran many tests and found out that my fallopian tubes were obstructed. They suggested doing a procedure where they try to flush them with a special liquid. *"I also strongly recommend that we remove the tubes if they are heavily obstructed and we cannot pass the fluid through,"* my doctor informed me. *"Well, doc,"* I looked at him and replied, *"It would be all good and fine but the issue is that I need to consult your findings with you before you start cutting anything out of me."*

I continued, *"I cannot just allow you to go in, do the job and possibly wake up being marked for the rest of my life. I would not be able to have a child ever. So for that reason, you will need to do your findings, close me up and when I wake up from anesthesia, we will have to discuss the next step."* My doctor looked shocked and warmed me, *"But you realize that we usually do that all at once. If the tubes are obstructed we need to remove them."* I was thinking how priceless humans and their organs truly are at that moment. I went for my procedure and, as my doctor had suspected, the tubes were obstructed. I was officially informed that I could no longer get pregnant naturally. It was devastating news to my family and me. I became depressed.

The only option was to try in vitro fertilization. I knew it was the only chance. We started to plan for it. I just had one more business trip to China. When I returned, I would be scheduling to get me pregnant. It was exciting! I was able to relax. We had a plan B. I stopped living in sadness. I could see the light at the end of the tunnel. I had a successful trip but started to feel horribly sick.

Even after I got home, it didn't get any better. I was thinking to myself that maybe I had caught the bird flu or a very bad bug in China. I went to see my doctor. *"Well, ma'am, you got a completely different type of 'bug' inside you,"* started my doctor. *"Congratulations, you are pregnant!"* I stared at him, shocked. *"It cannot be! No way!"* I realized I was screaming through the tears that had started to run down my cheeks. *"How can I be pregnant when they told me my fallopian tubes are blocked and I cannot get pregnant naturally?"* I asked him. *"The body is a miracle and works in a mysterious way,"* replied my family doctor.

Parents Worst Nightmare

"Everything connects to everything else."

-*Leonardo DaVinci*

Since my baby was born, I had a scary feeling deep inside of me. I could not figure out what it was but I could feel danger. I could not sleep well at night. I would be always coming to his room to check on him. My nights were interrupted. I lived with anxiety. My son did not have any major health issues but from time to time, he would come up with high fevers out of nowhere. We went to see many doctors and they would tell us to treat him with the usual Tylenol to reduce the fever. My motherly instinct, however, was telling me that there was something else going on.

"Why would the body induce fever out of the nowhere?" I could not stop questioning myself. I was pushing on the doctors to figure it out but they had no answers for me. They had no clue nor was it something they ever studied. It was very frustrating to me. Then one day my worst nightmare came true.

My son was only six. He was playing outside with his friends in front of our house and came inside to lay down in my office because he got tired. I didn't think much of it. He was warm and laid down on the floor as he has done many times before. In about ten minutes, I heard a strange sound. He was always a joker and center of attention. He played many times a game on me that he was dying, drowning or other such similar games. It always made me so mad when he did that. *"He must be playing the same game on me,"* I thought to myself. Something, however, was telling me to turn my back and check on him. He looked okay but there was something out of norm.

I could see saliva coming out of his mouth – something similar he had also done to me before. But this time it was different. I stood up from my desk and went towards him on the floor. He was shaking. His eyes were rolling back. I had never seen anything like that. I knew it was not good. *"Baby, what's going on?"* I started to scream hysterically. He was not responding. It was not another one of his games this time. He was having a seizure. I knew nothing about it and I didn't know what to do. I picked the phone and called 911.

I felt so frightened and thought it must be a nightmare I would wake up from at any given moment. This cannot be happening. I picked my baby up. I was holding him in my arms. He was turning blue. *"I am losing my child. This cannot be real,"* were my thoughts rushing through my brain. It was surreal and one of the most frightening moments of my life. My heart was rushing like never before. I had never done CPR. It was my motherly instinct that told me what to do. I had no idea what I was doing. I didn't know if I was doing it properly. It was just my dying child and me. I felt so hopeless and alone as if I was fighting the entire world.

"Where is the darn 911 ambulance," was my voice screaming inside of me. *"Why is it taking them so long?"* I was thinking while doing CPR. Then, finally, his body stopped getting blue. He started to gain his normal color back. I could see him breathing. He opened his eyes. I felt like I met my son for the first time again. My body was filled with the most amazing, warm feeling. I knew that he will be okay. I don't know when the ambulance arrived but it had to be at least ten minutes later.

My son was rushed to the hospital. The doctors diagnosed him with a febrile seizure. *"It does happen to children,"* explained the doctor. *"However, it usually happens to children under the age of six. He is bit older to have such symptoms but he is okay now. There is nothing to worry about,"* assured the doctor. *"Nothing to worry about? What about if I was not around to save him?"* I argued.

"What causes febrile seizure, doctor?" was my argument. I was trying to make some sense out of it. *"We do not really know. It is a reaction to high body temperature but we do not know why the body does that,"* was his reply. *"So, how can you say that he will be okay?"* I continued. *"Well, we can put him on strong steroids to make sure this does not repeat,"* was the doctor's reply.

I knew at that point that they are completely clueless and not even trying to make any sense of their own nonsense. I realized that my child was just a number in the statistic. *"How can they treat him with steroids when they do not even know where is the disease coming from?"* I was thinking as my blood pressure was increasing. I was outraged. I was very upset. I could not imagine my life without my precious baby. I felt absolutely no compassion. My son was just one of the many. What my child and I went through was just regular day at work for the doctors. I knew that since I brought my child to this world it was my responsibility to get to the bottom of it. I could not just let this go. I cannot depend on people who have no explanation. I felt like a lioness protecting her cub. For the following couple of years, I was like a hawk around my son. I started to research everything there was possible to start making some sense out of his sudden fevers and the horrifying episode. It was all part of my health mission.

As with my body, my son's fragile little body was also toxic and acidic. The sudden fevers were caused by inflammation in his body. That is how his body was reacting. It was sending us clear signals. All we had to do was to listen and help his body heal.

When I put all the pieces of the puzzle together, the entire family adopted clean lifestyle. Understanding what makes the body thrive and what makes the body build a disease was crucial. It was all about creating a healthy, alkaline body setting without an inflammation. We were on a mission. It was incredible to see the immediate results. Like magic, my son's fevers and health issues disappeared in just short few weeks.

I know if it was not for my natural instinct my little baby would be on heavy medications causing a host of other health issues. Or even worse he could not be even here. The medical system would get him into their claws early. They would have created a consumer out of him early on, which would have lasted for his lifetime for sure. I emphasize this because that is how the medical industry creates their customers. They grab them early on. What an injustice.

My son is a strong and thriving boy today. He takes no medication and I am so happy that I fought for him as any mother should for her children.

The Art of Parenting

"It took me four years to paint like Raphael, but a lifetime to paint like a child."

-*Pablo Picasso*

I felt terrified deep inside when I became a mother for the first time. There was so much pressure and so many expectations. Everything was new to me; I did not know how to process it all at once. I had no clue what to do. It felt like endless responsibilities were possibly expected of me. It was not only my life that I had to figure out, but now I was also responsible for someone else's life. I felt tremendous pressure and heaviness within me. To say that I felt stressed would be an understatement. I was tense and worried. I felt completely lost. I was constantly second-guessing myself. I was doubting myself and everything I was doing. I was comparing myself with other mothers. I was feeling that all the other parents had it under control except me. I felt like the only one, always behind on something.

There were baby playgroups to join. There were mommies' groups to join. There were doctors' appointments. There were scheduled vaccinations. The list was boundless. At the same time, I was also working at my demanding job. I was so lost that I decided to just go with the flow. I decided to accept *what is*. I was going to follow the natural flow of my inner motherhood's guidance. I followed my motherly instinct by feeding my babies when they were hungry. I was putting them to sleep when they were tired. I made them my own food. When we met other children at the park, we played. When we did not, we never felt the need to seek out others.

We think that our children are like us. The truth, however, is that while they did come into this world through us, they have come here to live their own life. They came here to be their own person. They did not come here to become a little copy of us nor did they come here to fulfill any of our unfulfilled dreams. Our children are their own person. They are a unique spark of light that the world has never seen before. Their only job is to spread this light and create something unique. The worst thing to do is to make them fit into some pre-calculated form. It dulls their sparkle. This also creates a pressure, not only for them but also for you, as you want them to be someone they are not.

It is everything else that you were taught to believe. Your child is already amazing in her own unique way. She is more than enough. She is magical, inspiring, and pure intelligence. She is uncontaminated. She is absolutely pure and divine. Your child can teach you so much about life. If you ever feel lost in life, have a talk with a three year old. She will explain life to you with an incredible wonder in her eyes. She will show you magical things everywhere. She will put things into perspective and show you how to make sense of life again. She will simplify not only life but also your problems for you. Life will make sense again.

"Mom, it is amazing what a few minutes can mean in your life," said my youngest son, when we were driving to go grocery shopping. He was referring to the great surfing experience he'd had a day ago. He was only

thirteen but already a great surfer. *"I caught this perfect wave and I rode the whole thing. It was only a few minutes but it was the most incredible feeling in the world."*

There was so much excitement radiating from my son as he told me about his feelings. He was so tuned in and aware of himself and the feeling of high that he had experienced. *"I am so happy for you but please always be very careful,"* I replied as a typical worrisome mom over her baby. *"I know. I have to respect the ocean and go with its flow. Never against it,"* continued my son. *"You are so right. You must respect it and go with its flow. Resistance is never good in anything you do. You must always be aligned with the things around you to maintain your inner peace and strength,"* I agreed. It made me proud to see that he was growing into a conscious and self-aware person.

My children never ceased to surprise me. They were always very observant and aware. It was due to their direct upbringing but they had also involuntarily become part of my own journey to awakening. It was always very important for me to give my children the best education and knowledge possible. What I am referring to is not the schooling they receive from the establishment but the wisdom and experience that we can pass on to them. Teaching them about health and how to prevent disease. We must teach them how to use food as their only medicine. They need to know how to honor their body as a divine gift and holy temple. Their wellbeing is the number one priority and we need to teach them how to take care of it and make it their responsibility. They need to learn how to respect nature and all its beings. Every being has the same right to life as they do; no one is superior or inferior. Lastly, they need to be taught how to be honest and true to themselves. We must teach them to always speak their truth and to be true to who they really are.

Your child is an absolute emptiness, a void, filled with an infinite vibrational intelligence of the Universe. He brings unimaginable wisdom and potential, which this world has not yet seen. He is in tune with the nature and he attains knowledge by relying on his own instinct. The establishment knows this; it fears his innate knowledge and strength. It fears that if your child's intelligence is left on its own, he will not conform. He will continue to be his own infinite being that can think on his own. The establishment fears his independent thinking, and his independent being. The system is afraid that he can never become a slave. He will never be conformed into a structure of domination and manipulation. He is free and for that, he is seen as a pure rebel. His innocence needs to be broken right away. His wings must be cut off. He then receives a wheelchair to be rolled around in and permanently become dependent.

We, the parents, are the same children, so we naturally continue in the same way as our parents raised us. We say, we want our children to live independently, but unconsciously we do exactly the opposite. We make our children dependent. Our children conform to the well-calculated rules and conditions of the system. We feel good to be the master and have obedience. Finally, we have a purpose, something worth living for. What this does in truth is that it creates a resistance. Any resistance is an unnatural force. We are no longer a fluid flow of unconditional love but a law enforcement. Nothing good can ever come from force, which is why we need to adopt a different way of teaching. We need to influence our children through their own creativity. We need to encourage their independent thinking. We need to excite their inner genius and let their spark glow. We need to bring oxygen to their fire. We need to step down from a role of a police officer and step into a role of a friend, who is a child himself. A child that is the same student of life as our children are.

There is a hidden genius within each child and it is our job to help discover that genius. We need to observe our children and understand their inner world. We need to immerse ourselves into it. Everybody sees children as stupid; we assume children don't know anything. We need to teach them because we see children as incomplete beings. We only see them. We never truly listen to them because we supposedly know better. We think that because we are a doctor, professor or a parent we know everything. We create a superiority and a barrier, which is impossible to climb over. We discredit our children and refuse to respect them as our equals. We have unconsciously reduced them to nothing. Children became the most exploited class in our society. We have unknowingly enslaved our children.

This is why our world is in such utter chaos. This impels thousands of children to commit suicide each year. This chaotic state also inspires hundreds of children to be more violent. They take a gun and go to school to shoot their friends and teachers. Then, we sit there, wondering what the world has come to.

Our children are trying to tell us something very important. They are literally screaming at us for help but no one is listening. Instead, we think there needs to be more armed forces in front of the school and more poisonous suicide-causing antidepressant prescriptions. We think that guns are the problem without realizing that someone still has to pull the trigger. Guns do not kill on their own. Our children are trying to tell us that they've had enough! Our children are tired of being treated like mental slaves in the lowest class of society. They want to be respected. Our children want to be understood. They simply want to be given permission for being children instead of instant adults. Our children want to feel like they matter.

Our children are brilliant. They are like sponges that absorb everything they see and hear around them. They are a fertile soil. It is our job to plant beautiful flowers instead of weeds into their minds. It is our job as parents and teachers to equip them for life with the truth. Life presents a lot of wonderful challenges and opportunities. It is our duty to make our children strong and resilient to overcome them. We have to help them build their own strength. We have to encourage them to think for themselves. We can never underestimate their natural intelligence. We need to make them connected to their natural roots so that they can feel and be in touch with whom they are. We need to help them unleash the supernatural. We need to let their unlimited power and energy shine through. It is our job to make them feel the unconditional love everywhere. To see life as an amazing blessing and problems as invitation to only become better. Teach them to be always true to themselves because they are enough and always will be.

To show them how to keep their hearts open and know how to love. Show them that it is ok to be vulnerable at times because that is what makes them human. Show them how to not only share but also master their thoughts, feelings and emotions. Be proud of them and teach them love for nature and all the creatures that have the same right to live as we do. Show them that it is perfectly fine to be unique in their own special way. Allow them to pursue their passion and follow their heart. Allow them to make their own mistakes so that they can learn and grow from them.

We, as parents, need to stop being so over worried for them and their destiny. Each person can only know his or her own journey. It is not our job to find someone else's journey. We cannot hinder them from growing and going places that they need to travel through. It is their journey not ours.

They will be fine like you are fine at the present. The more freedom you give them, the stronger individuals they will become. When you allow them to do this, you allow them to establish peace within, learn from their own actions and build responsibility over their destiny. This will enable them to find their own way. In this way, they will be true to their higher intelligence. They will connect to their super consciousness that knows the truth. Their consciousness naturally knows the difference between good and bad.

Take a deep breath and relax because nothing is under your control. We are all in good hands. Let go and trust that everything will be perfectly fine at the end. If it is not fine, then it could only mean that this is not the end. The fact that children are still being born to this world of war and conflict is a reminder that the Universe has not given up on us. It is a reminder that there is still faith in the human kind. It is a hope that we will wake up from our dark psychosis.

Children are the most precious gift, they are a divine treasure. Our children are the future and our only hope for a better world. It is time to start our evolution into the kind beings we are meant to be. It is time to unite and embrace in love, which is the only salvation of this broken world.

Education

> "If you judge fish by its ability to climb a tree it will always remain thinking it is stupid."
>
> *-Albert Einstein*

School was never designed for me. I went to school with fear. I had a fear from failing and not being the best for my parents. That inner fear foundation proliferated into anything that had to do with traditional schooling. The educational establishment only supported the fear-based, cookie-cutting ideology. I had a fear of most of my teachers. If it were up to me I would have never gone there. Even the building had a weird smell and the energies were off. It was depressing there. I was sensitive to the entire vibe. Going to school was a torture.

The whole process of mass education was stressing me to the point that I could not sleep at night. The mental anguish started to reflect also on my health. I was getting sick very often. I used every trick to skip the school. *"Mom, my stomach hurts and I feel like I am going to vomit. My head hurts also badly,"* I would say right as my mom had to rush to see her patients. I learned a lot about the symptoms from my doctor mother that I would use into my advantage. I had to learn how to work the system.

The more I would be thinking about the symptoms I would actually start feeling them. It was almost scary to see the power of my thoughts and how my body would follow like an obedient servant. *"Oh, no you must be coming down with the flu,"* my mom would say. It gave me a ticket to stay home from school at least for a few days. It was like a little vacation from the scary place I had to go to every day. I had my friends to visit me after school. They would bring me my homework and I had a blast. I studied everything in half the time or less than the time I would be sitting behind a desk at school. The rest was for the things I wanted to do. I would draw. I would create a new outfit. I would take care of my fish. I would sit by the window and watch the nature. I daydreamed a lot. I was absorbing the present moment. I was spending time with me. I was indulging in my complete silence. I was being happy for no specific reason. I loved my little *"vacations"*. I took as many of them as it was possible without being expelled. I loved spending time with myself. I had a great time with me. I was feeling connected with everything. There was such stillness and yet I felt so alive through a movement within me. I felt alive.

I never really understood school. I never quite understood what they were trying to achieve there. We were all different kids and I felt how they are trying to make us all the same. Since little kid I knew that I do not fit. I was different. The harder I tried to fit in the more difficult it became not only for me but also those around me. The schooling concept was stressing me. To avoid school as much as possible I faked all kinds of diseases. I even faked such stomach pains that it resulted in my appendix to be removed. It was a product of my thoughts.

I was into science and languages. I absolutely hated history and chemistry. It was mainly due to the teachers I had. My history teacher was an interesting lady. She was in her mid-fifties and single. Her father was some famous history professor and it looked as he married her off to her profession. She looked like she reincarnated from some ancient times and didn't have time to adjust. She was not only disconnected from us but her own existence as well. I feared mass education and especially the testing system. I could not take tests. My brain would freeze. The school system made me feel stupid and such a waste. It was making me think that I will probably never accomplish to be anything. It was a miracle that I made it out of there with honors. None of it, however, was accomplished through a love for knowledge but purely out of fear. What a waste of precious years.

The entire education establishment is designed around memorization. It is not about intelligence or creativity. It is about loading information and facts into the brain to turn man into a robot. It is literally loading the subconscious mind with programming to turn you into a computer. Our schools and universities are computer production lines. It is about how good you can memorize useless information that you will ninety percent of time never need. And if you end up needing it you know where to find it.

Today's advanced digital age of Internet has anything at your fingertips in a split of a second. School makes you memorize information so that you can take a test. Your head is loaded with a useless nonsense to spit it out for even more meaningless test. The better you can spit the better grades you get. There is only one objective. You have to memorize the information exactly as it is. You cannot use your own critical thinking to add anything. You cannot use your own intelligence to delete anything. You cannot be creative. You cannot be ingenious. You cannot be innovative. You cannot think outside of the box. You must stay in the box!

This kind of approach kills the genius within. It does not encourage you to be creative and invent new things that have not been seen yet. It reduces you to a mere programmed machine. You waste twenty years and thousands of dollars to become a robot. Congratulations! Once you are a robot, it becomes extremely difficult to rewire your programming back to human again. That is why we have such a high rise of stress and head related problems ranging from headaches to depression. That is why we see such a rise of addiction and suicide not only among adults but among children as well. That is why we find ourselves in such a chaos.

We think nothing of that and like the good robots we are we go on to prescribe anti-depressants that only further mess up the brain. The truth is your brain has a hard time to process the duality and artificial intelligence you have become. You no longer feel real anymore. You lost a connection with your heart and live in your head. It gets very noisy and loud in there. Your brain goes nonstop and you do not know how to turn it off. You do not know what is going on. You become your own prison.

This is a crazy world we have created for ourselves. It is time to see the truth. It is time to pause and rethink our way of being. Human kind needs to evolve and the right type of education is needed in order to achieve that. There are only two paths you can take. You can be an enslaved robot or you can become a person of a great wisdom and freedom. It is crucial to remember if you decide to take the first route it is rather crowded there. There are lot of robots out there and it becomes more and more difficult to be a special robot among the millions. Or the other option is that you embark on a path less traveled. You remove yourself from the herd. It is only the asleep sheep that keeps marching with the herd.

Once you remove yourself, you become free to go wherever you would like to. It is pretty much guaranteed you will become very knowledgeable and wise. It will not be a repeated knowing of others but your own gained knowledge through your discoveries and experiences. You will no longer be a parrot who knows how to repeat but you will become an eagle going high for the sky. The higher you go the smaller those on the ground will appear. You will become creative. You will become confident. You will become revolutionary. You will become intelligence itself.

When you step aside from the herd, you become your own person. You become an individual. You are no longer part of the Republican herd. You are no longer part of the Democratic herd. You are no longer part of the American herd. You are You! You are your own party. You are your own self-governed individual who knows the difference between right and wrong. You are your own individual who does not need to be told how and what to think. You become an individual who can use his own intelligence and create the reality of his dreams. You will no longer be a slave to other's ideologies.

Only an individual can awaken. Only an individual can be enlightened. Crowd can never become enlightened. You will have to be brave. You will have to be bold to be revolutionary. You will have to be self-disciplined to walk alone. You will have to be ready to be alone and love your own company. You will have to love yourself. You will have to travel deep within yourself to connect to your super consciousness. You will have to find your higher intelligence. You will have to reach the center of your very own being. This center of your existence will then connect you with the entire Universe. This is what you have been searching for your entire life.

This is the birth to your true self. The true self understands the fact that the Earth has been here for 4.6 billions of years and we will never discover all there is to discover. It is the understanding that science is truly a field of uncertainty until we discover something new that will prove how incorrect we were in the past. Humanity since its conception has sent itself on a hunt of trying to know everything but the truth is that we cannot arrive at point where we will know it all. The more we learn and know the more we realize how little we actually know and how much more there is yet to know and discover. You can get lost in all the knowledge and might not realize that too much of knowing is actually further removing you from life enjoyment itself. Unlearn all that you have been taught. Learn to use your natural instinct and your inner wisdom. Learn to listen to your heart because simplicity is the highest level of sophistication.

Attachment

> "Attachment is the root of all suffering."
> *-Buddha*

When you were born you came into this life experience. You came alone and alone you will leave. That is the truest truth. There is no other way around it. You will never again be a part of anyone else in a true physical form. You might carry a new life within you if you become a mother but you personally will never be a part of anyone else ever again. You will no longer be attached to anyone else and this is the root of your problem. You want to belong. You want to be attached to something, to someone. You want to feel whole again. You miss the feeling of belonging and being part of something bigger. You miss the feeling of being secure and completely protected as you were in your mother's womb. There is not another place like that. The nourishment was coming without you even thinking. You were protected and floating in an ocean of love.

The loving tender care was everywhere around you. It was the perfect temperature and the perfect setting. It was tranquil. There was no stress. There were no worries. You were loved unconditionally. You were just allowed to be. You were allowed to be yourself without any prejudice or judgment. It was a heaven you have experienced and you want it back.

Then one day you were pushed out. You were pushed out from the loving place of safety into a cold unknown place of uncertainty. You cried and wanted to go back. There were strange sounds. There were strange colors and strange tastes. It was hectic and busy. There was no tranquility. There was a lot of stress everywhere. Everyone was rushing somewhere and everyone was worried about something. It was scary. You stood there with your eyes wide open in an awe not understanding what does it mean for you. You went on living your life with hopes that you will find the same sense of belonging again. You were made believe that it must be somewhere out there through some kind of material possession or relationship experience. You have been accumulating things and people only to realize that it is not there.

Your false sense of attachment has become the root of all your suffering. The truth is that once you left your mother's womb you are in this life experience all by yourself and you own nothing. You came here empty handed and empty handed you will also return. You can never truly own anything. You can have a house. You can have a car. You can have shoes. You can have furniture. These are only material things. Even these things come and go. House can be lost. Furniture can burn. Car can be stolen or crashed into pieces. Shoes will be worn out. Even these priced possessions will not last forever nor will you take them with you when you die. They are here for you to enjoy them but not to obsess over them nor to get attached to them. These things are not what makes who you are.

The same is with people. You can never own a person. Your parents do not own you and you do not own your parents. Your spouse does not own you. You do not own your spouse. You do not even own your children. All beings are only their own, living their own life and walking their own journey. You can never own these people, you can only love them. It is very important to understand it. It might be upsetting. It might be scary or even frightening. It is, however, time to accept the absolute truth.

You are a free agent. Once you left your mother's womb, you became a completely independent being. You became free. There is no turning back. You are a free person and aloneness is your natural state. Aloneness is the only form of true freedom. It is a freedom from anything including your thoughts that are making you believe that if you are not attached you are a failure, not loved and unworthy individual. Being alone is all there is and aloneness is what you are. You can no longer crawl into another being and for that, it is critical to understand the meaning of aloneness. You must understand what being alone means. You need to learn about it so that you can embrace it rather than fear it. You must learn how to celebrate it, enjoy it, and master it. No matter how much we try to deny we will forever be alone. Being alone, however, does not mean to feel lonely. There is a fundamental difference between these two states.

There is a common misunderstanding between aloneness and loneliness. Being alone is not the same as being lonely. Loneliness means that you are missing something. You are missing someone. You are not complete. You are feeling a void of some kind. Loneliness means that you are not fulfilled. You are not fully satisfied and for that you are searching to find something to satisfy you. You are searching for someone to make you feel good. You are searching for someone to rescue you from your misery. Loneliness is your mind not being at peace. It is your mind constantly chasing some type of pleasure in order to feel fully satisfied. Feeling lonely is your mind not at ease. Your mind is dis-eased.

We suffocated ourselves in activities to avoid boredom arising from loneliness. We filled ourselves with all kinds of things to avoid ourselves.

You go to a movie theater. You go to a baseball game. You go to a bar. You go to a dinner. You go to look for a partner. You go to the beach. You follow a leader. You meditate. You go to pray and worship some idea or belief. You go on the Internet to seek more knowledge. You go to work out to make yourself tired to stop the mind thinking how lonely you are. You are constantly seeking an activity of some sort to avoid boredom. Our entire civilization is built on an escape of some sort.

We fear to be bored because there is no one to entertain us. Being bored means that you have nothing to do. Being bored means that you must be quite and still. Being quite and still terrifies you because it would require to look within. You are horrified to look within because you fear that there will be nothing to find. You fear it will be an empty space because you do know that it is an empty space. You are afraid to go there. You are afraid of the darkness and the unknown. It becomes a sense of inexhaustible pain that you cannot escape although you try so very hard to get away from it.

Being alone is not easy. It requires an extraordinary intelligence to be alone. It is the mind that does not want to allow you to be alone. The mind races like a car on a speedway looking for any kind of escape. The mind is edgy and tries to fill itself with knowledge and things. That is how you are. That is your way of modern existence. You have been living like this for many years, filling yourself with activities, relationships, and experiences. The question remains if you have succeeded to fill the void, the empty space yet?

You can only fill the void and stop your loneliness when you stop escaping. To stop escaping you need to take a trip within yourself. You will find out that your magnificent body is made of over seventy trillion cells. These trillions of cells are made of molecules that are made of atoms. Each atom is 99% an empty space. If you would take an actual trip through your body on a microscopic level, travel through your amazing system like a curious explorer and upon your return would tell us what you saw; you would be stunned to report that you saw absolutely nothing. You would tell us that there is absolutely nothing within you. You would tell us there was only an empty space.

Think of your body like a smartphone. It is a standalone device, not physically connected to anything but yet it is somehow able to receive all kinds of information and connect you with millions of people across the globe. Your smartphone receives e-mails. It receives pictures of your friends from across the globe and it sends pictures back to them. It allows you to talk and see people in real time. It allows you to produce money and watch the stock market. It shows you how to make a delicious recipe or how to build a car. How is it possible? How does this small device accomplish such things? Whether it is a cellular phone, microwave or radio they receive and transmit signals. It depends on the wavelength and the frequency what kind of transmission is received. Your cellular phone receives and transmits electromagnetic waves. These kinds of waves are much larger than the wavelengths of the kind of light that can be detected by a human eye.

It is the same *emptiness* that delivers information into your smartphone that you communicate your existence with the Universe. It is a back and forth continuous communication. You are like that smartphone. While it might appear you are completely disconnected and alone, you are not. You are always connected to the same *emptiness* of the Universe that is not empty at all. It is filled with all information there is. It is the world wide web of real intelligence. You are the place of connection that communicates with everything around you and through you. You are an irreplaceable part of the Divine Matrix. Everything is connected to everything. Nothing is separately standing alone in some kind of magical vacuum, including you.

Energy is all that our world is made of. You are also made of the same energy. Energy, vibration and frequency – that is your world. It is what makes this world go around. It is only energy that creates the forms you can see through your naked eye and feel through experiences such as taste, smell or touch. This energy holds everything together. Even the chair you are sitting on is really not even there. You are not even sitting on it but slightly floating above it. To make sense out of our existence and everything around we need to evolve our thinking. We need ascend the eye-deceiving perception.

We need to understand that our five senses do not share the entire world with us. They are indeed very limited and leave so much left out. There is so much more we do not see. In fact, what we can experience through our senses is only a very limited spectrum of wavelengths available in the space around us. We can only experience one trillionth of the electromagnetic spectrum. As a result, we experience reality that is only partial due to a limited biology of our senses and our beliefs.

Knowing that you are almost one hundred percent an empty space brings a very important question. What does it mean? How can we understand it? And more importantly how can we master it? Let's take a look at a tree. A tree is not floating in the middle of the air somewhere. Its roots need to be planted in the soil. It needs to get water in order to live. It needs sunshine in order to prosper. It needs the air to function. And we need the trees. Without them we cannot survive. You are like that tree. You might not have the same roots but you cannot function without the soil that gives you food. You cannot function without the sunshine that delivers crucial energy that makes your food through photosynthesis you need to live and thrive. You cannot function without the air. You are no different from the tree. You depend on your outer world and the outer world depends on you. You are part of the entire eco-system no matter if you like it or not. You might fight it and ignore it but the fact will always remain that you cannot function without it.

Like every cell in your body is accounted for and needed, the same is true for you. You are part of the Divine Matrix, the Creation itself. It is the invisible web of energy flow that holds everything together. It is the 'emptiness' everywhere around you that is not empty at all. It is filled with sacred information.

Imagine it like an endless sky. It is there but you cannot touch nor put it into your pocket. The same beautiful emptiness is inside of you. Take the sky and everything beyond and put it inside of you. Fill yourself with all there is. You are so very empty and yet filled completely with the endless supply of energy and flow that can never make you feel empty once you train your brain to comprehend it. You are the stillness with movement dancing within you.

Close your eyes and imagine the energies dancing within you. Imagine you are leaving the room you are in. Imagine you are leaving the building you are in. Imagine leaving the town you are in. The state you are in. The country you are in. The continent you are in. Imagine you are leaving the planet and keep going. It is an endless, infinite eternity you enter. The infinite eternity is filling you, one organ at a time, every cell, every molecule. Feel the infinite energy filling your entire body, your entire existence. Feel the Universe rushing through your veins, your arteries, your heart and all that you are. This is you. You are the Universe and the Universe is you.

Keep taking these excursions as often as you like until you do not have to even think about it. It becomes natural and part of your connection between your inner and outer world. You will learn to understand that there is no physical barrier. You are connected to everything and everything is connected to you. You are never unaccompanied. You are always connected to an amazing web of creation and for that you can never be lonely. You will open the gates to become everything. You will take down the invisible, yet so limiting walls of feeling alone and being separated. You will re-establish the long lost connection. You will become One.

The Art of Dying

> "To understand this world, you have to think in terms of energy, frequency and vibration."
>
> -*Nikola Tesla*

My grandma and I were very close. She was like a second mother to me. She was my mentor. Even though she did not have a college degree, grandma had a worldly intelligence. Her wisdom was captivating and astounding. She was interested in life and the Universe. She studied the sky, stars and nature. My grandma was a world of knowledge. She taught me how to love nature and all of its beings. She had an amazing energy around her. She was my sacred place, where I could store all of my secrets, wishes and dreams. My grandma was a sanctuary; there was peace and harmony in her presence. She never judged or condemned me for the way I was. She taught me about forgiveness and acceptance. My grandma was one of the most beautiful, divine beings that I have ever met. Love permeated through her and she empowered me with unconditional love.

She lived a simple but rich life. My grandma would only eat if she was hungry and she'd usually eat small meals that were made from real food. She would sleep for plenty of hours in the night and rest in the afternoon by taking naps. My grandma would spend time outside to get sunshine and fresh air. She moved and stretched her body daily because she was mindful of her being. Rather than wasting, she conserved anything, whenever possible. My grandma was always there for everyone and we all loved to be around her.

Our entire family has been grateful for every single day we got to spend with her. My grandma was the glue to our entire family through her wisdom and peace. The thought of losing her one day was horrifying me for years, as she got older. I was so worried about the day I'll no longer be able to touch her or hear her voice. I feared the day that I will not be able to visit her. She was such an important part of my life. She was everything to me. In so many different ways, she shaped me into who I am today. She was such a huge influence for me that I could not imagine the world without her.

Nevertheless, I had to prepare myself for the inevitable. We all knew this was coming and I had to face the truth. I had to make my peace with the fact. It was also my inner voice urging me to make my final visit with my grandma to say goodbye. That's what my last trip to Europe was about, it was a farewell. It was a trip to give her one last hug and let her know that it will all be fine. I had to tell her that there is nothing to worry about nor anything to fear.

"Grandma, are you afraid of dying?" I asked her directly to start our necessary conversation. I have always felt a strong spiritual connection between us. It was a connection that we never talked about, but it was simply there. We both knew about it. We shared an unconditional love between our hearts. I knew this conversation about death was mandatory. I knew we can no longer pretend like it does not exist. I could feel my grandma thinking about it. I could feel her being distressed about death. I could feel her anxiety and fear. *"Yes, of course I am. It is not the death*

itself but the knowing that it will be the end and then nothing more." she answered. She was looking at me and I could see a scared child through her eyes. There was such an innocence and wonder in her eyes.

Death was the big unknown no one wanted to talk about. Our conversation was essential to create a bridge between her physical departure and our continued spiritual existence. Our existence that never ends, it just merely changes its form. Grandma and I had to create the bridge so that there is nothing left unspoken in our present life experience and only amazing new things to look forward to in the next existence. It was one of the most magical conversations we ever had. The best was left for the last.

Nothing Ends

> "Goodbyes are only for those who love with their eyes. Because for those who love with heart and soul there is no such thing as separation."
>
> *-Rumi*

Death is an unavoidable and inseparable part of life because without death there is no life. Everything has to die in order to be renewed again. Each day has to die for a new day to be born again. Each flower has to die for new buds to grow out again. Life is a continuum of renewals; there is no end to anything as long as there is life in this Universe.

What is it about death that makes you afraid? How can you be afraid of something you have not experienced? It might be possibly only the fear of the unknown. Being afraid of death is like being afraid to go to sleep. When you go to sleep, you fall into a state of unconsciousness.

Do you ever worry or fear going to sleep? I do not think so. To the contrary, I am sure you look forward to going to sleep. You want it, you need it and you certainly deserve it. The body requires a proper break after a long hard day at work or wherever your daily activities take you. At the end of the day, you must rest by going to sleep. The body needs to rejuvenate and recharge in order to renew. Every living being needs sleep. When you die, you make the same trip. In death, you enter into the same, beautiful, relaxing, light-filled state of unconsciousness.

The only difference between death and sleep is that you do not come back to the same bodily form. The body is worn out and a pain-filled shell that was left behind. The body that served its journey has gone to rest. However, your soul and your divine higher Self is filled with immortal unconditional love that keeps on living and embarks on a new journey. A new journey of your energy being transformed into the next form as Albert Einstein proved. He showed how energy cannot be created nor destroyed. Energy just changes from one form into another. It is the law of physics, *$E=mc^2$*.

Death is a part of life, it always was and always will be. You can deny this fact but you cannot escape it. You cannot ignore the truth nor can you be shocked by death. You cannot be offended when I tell you that *you will die one day* because death is inescapable. It is an inevitable part of our life. Eventually, I will die too and so will everyone else. Death shall not be a surprise because it is meant to happen. If you are ready to live, then you must also be ready to die. Only through death, immortality can be found. It is not the death that your mind is afraid of. Your mind is the ego, which is the false self. The death you are thinking of is the death of your false self. It is death of ego itself, which is why it makes you fear death so much. It is the ego fearing its own death, the death of your memories and experiences.

Immortality is in each dying moment because there is something new coming right after. In every minute, there is an end and a beginning. In every passing minute, there is eternity and in each minute, there is a renewal. In every minute, there is new excitement.

Dying is the finest art of all. It has no special motivation nor incentive to a person. Death brings absolutely no value to anyone. The only purpose of death is for life as a whole. We cannot escape death but we can escape the fear that creates the pain. We can escape the suffering and ease the sadness. We can relieve the sorrow that comes from death by understanding the truth. Accepting the truth, by making a conscious sense of death is paramount. It will give us the ability to make a bridge of consciousness between the living, the dying and the dead.

Most people fear death till the last moment until it finally happens. For that, most people die unconsciously. Their loved ones have the same fear since no one is willing to explore and understand the unavoidable. No one is able to accept their inevitable fate and learn the truth. This is why dying is such an art. This is why, it is needed for each man and each woman to learn the truth in order to make this transition consciously.

In order to reach the conscious sense of death there cannot be fear. There can be only unconditional love, which requires staying mindful and aware throughout the process of death. You need this unconditional love to make the bridge that grants freedom from sorrow and suffering. It liberates an individual from regret and pity.

Unconditional love frees you from misery. This love is the bridge between the living and the dying. You can always die on your own, alone and in despair. Or you can turn the misery into a blissful experience. You can make this transitional trip beautiful. You can make it mindful and joyous. You can make it exciting. You can make it ecstatic. Instead of being alone and full of fear, you can be surrounded by others sharing the same joy with you through the awareness and in the presence of unconditional love.

The choice is yours.

Chapter 6

LOVE

> "I love you neither with my heart, nor my mind. My heart might stop, my mind can forget. I love you with my soul because my soul never stops or forgets."
>
> -*Rumi*

What Love Is Not

What is love? Love is everything that love is not as we know it today. In order to bring clarity to something that we all want and are searching for, in order to understand what love is, we first need to understand what it is not. We need to understand the familiar before we can understand the unfamiliar.

What does it mean when you say to somebody that you love them? Usually, you do not say it until there is some kind of intimate relation established. Have you noticed? In these days, many people have no problem giving each other their bodies but to give love is a very difficult task. Love is the most exclusive and hidden treasure that has gone missing. We all feel it deep within ourselves but to give it away is not easy at all. To admit love and say, *"I love you"* is a cumbersome process. It usually takes weeks or even months before the person of interest tells you that. Sometimes the person you are seeing never tells you. Your relationship is a pure sex exchange because you are both needy.

Why is that? Is it because most people might be afraid of love? It must be so. What they are afraid of is being vulnerable and possibly, of not getting the same love in return. They are afraid that if they tell their person that they love them, they might not feel the same. They fear rejection. They fear certain obligation that can fall on them if they give their love. Love has become a business. Love has become a pure transaction. If I give you love, I want to ensure you give me the same amount of love back and things that are missing in my life. This is not love.

Love has become emotional. Love has become tied to emotions and for that reason; it is a very shaky business. Love has become a loveless emotion. You say you love your boyfriend. You say you love your teacher. You say you love your neighbor. The moment that the person of interest fails to make you feel good or fails to perform according to your liking, your *"love"* for them turns into hate. All of this happens in a matter of seconds. This is not love.

Once you receive the "I love you" confirmation, your mind makes you think that you own that person. From that ownership, jealousy arises. You are afraid of losing the person. You are afraid to lose a source of pleasure. You are afraid to lose a source of self-worth. You are afraid to lose a source of self-validation. You are afraid to feel lost, lonely, and empty. This is not love but merely obsession.

Love is the most highly prized currency. There is nothing more valuable or powerful than love. When there is jealousy, possession, envy, fear or hate there can be no love. It is only a product of the mind. There is only one type of love. It is not that you love your parents one way, your children another and your spouse yet completely different way. Love is only one. It is a universal force of life and it is unconditional. That type of love does not possess. That love does not envy. That love does not fear. That love does not hate.

You cannot teach someone to love. You cannot practice love. Any such activities are functions of the mind. Love is when you ascend your mind and quiet down your thinking. Love is when you stop fearing. Love is when you see yourself in the other. Love is when you trust and surrender to what is because you know you are in good hands. You know that the Universe has your back. When you love, it is not that you love this being or that being. Love is universal. When you love, you love all there is. When you love, you build a bridge between yourself and all there is. When you love, you become one with the whole Universe.

Tough Love

> "The purpose of pain is to move us into action; it is not to make us suffer."
>
> *- Tony Robbins*

My mom and dad were tough parents. They were strict, especially my mom. My mom was tough and firm with my sister and I but when it came to others, she was simply the life of the party. She loved company. As a medical doctor she was always surrounded by a lot of people. She was a people's person. Her profession was not about medicine but people. Her patients were not numbers. She cared about each of them as though they were family members. They were all important to her. They all mattered to her on a personal level.

It has never seized to surprise me how welcoming she was to everyone. She would be in the middle of cleaning the windows when the bell would ring. She would literally drop everything and invite visitors inside. She was quite the hostess. In no time, she would whip up an amazing meal for her guests. She would be full of glowing, welcoming, and entertaining vitality. My mom was amazing. No wonder people always wanted to drop in and hang around our place. My mom loved to entertain and she liked having tons of people around.

While she was super sweet to others, her love towards me was tough. I never quite understood it but I subconsciously knew that she did that to raise me a strong individual. I knew she was raising me to be ready to deal with the world. She wanted to ensure that I was ready to take on any life challenges that will come along the way. I think she knew that my journey will not be easy. My parents had to get me ready. My mom and dad were raising a warrior.

I was never pampered in love. I was not told that I am loved. I was never afforded much of loving emotions as far as I can remember. My parents would jump into a fire for me. I could absolutely count on both of them but there was something missing. Something important was not there. I could see their love through their actions rather than affections.

There was a mysterious, unspoken energy between us that we shared; I only wished we could tap into it. I could only see it as I was growing up that other parents were possibly more sensitive with their children. I secretly envied them. My parents showed their dedication through their actions. I knew I was always supported. There was no question about that. There was, however, never a lot of sweet and compassionate words in my life that came from my parents. It was rather a strength-building mechanism that they used. It made me feel like I was in military training many times. I leaned on my faith knowing that I had dedicated parents. I knew they wanted only the best for me. For that reason, I had to accept *what is* and their unique way of loving.

My mom and dad were always there for me in any situation that I needed them. I knew that they would always have my back and that was important to me. I only wished that we had a closer emotional connection. I wished I could let them into my inner world so they could make sense of my life and my purpose. There was something that was blocking this from happening, though. I did not know what it was until I found out the details of what they had to do to prevent me from being a handicap. I learned how hard they had to fight for my wellbeing. They had to fight not only me but also the external world that was so judgmental.

My parents were labeled as *"bad"* people by so many because of my therapy. They had to gather all their strength to withstand the criticism. They went against their entire world. Their inner instinct and their higher intelligence, fueled by unconditional love, was giving them the needed faith, power and guidance to go through with it. They knew there was no other way. It was their unconditional love for their daughter that made them put me through torturous pain in order to heal. They sacrificed two years of their life, their days and nights, to give me the best start for my life. They knew they were building an amazing future for me. They knew that is the only future I deserved.

It did leave a pricey mark on us, however. It made it very difficult for my parents to let go of their guard. The strenuous years and pain created fear in them. It was a fear of whether or not everything will be okay at the end. It created a lifelong fear for my wellbeing. They could not let go of that fear and relax. It was now programmed into their minds. They did not know when it was safe to surrender and loosen up. Their entire body was consumed by fear and they became stiff. They did not know how to become fluid again. Their existence became stressed without them being even aware of it. Their sacrifice for my physical wellness affected our mental wellbeing.

They needed me to be tough and for that reason, toughness became their way of raising me. They did not know how to be vulnerable again. They could not show much affection and emotions. They became locked up. It left me puzzled for years and blocked my own connection toward them as well. I became an introvert while to the world, I acted as an extravert. It was all just a show and I was the greatest actress. It was all for the show to get the missing affection. I was living in resentment deep down. I did not know any of this until I started to look for myself. I was tired of my acting role. I had to return to my true self and heal all of my traumas in order to remove my blockage.

This happened when I finally learned about the detailed specifics about my birth and the torturous therapy I had to forgo thereafter. It was only then that I could fully understand not only myself but my parents as well. It was the induced physical pain that healed me but also separated me from my parents for most of my life. My subconscious programming associated them with pain and suffering. It was the obstacle I could feel between us but never knew where it was coming from. I had to release the hurt and resentment. I had to liberate myself from the resistance. I had to open my eyes to be able to find the good in the bad. I had to understand that the physical pain was for my greater good. I had to forgive. I had to replace the bitterness with love and gratitude.

I knew that things could have been done possibly differently and better but none of us are perfect. My parents were not perfect either but they did their best. They did all they could and for that reason, I had to see and acknowledge their unconditional love. I had to see myself in them. It was a surreal moment flooded with lot of tears. It was a beautiful release, though. I was cleansing my deeply stored anger and anguish. I was finally able to be free to thank them for their sacrifice and love them more than ever.

Interestingly enough, it also released a physical pain I was experiencing in my affected arm for years. I would get spasms in it from time to time. I was doing physical therapy, special exercises, and detox but nothing was helping me. It was years of pain that I had to live with. Once I released the mental pain, however, the physical pain completely cleared. It was entirely lifted and my right arm became stronger than ever.

It was tough love that was able to give me a life of a regular, healthy person. It was truth leading into unconditional love that unleashed the supernatural powers within me to become all that I dreamed to be. As my mother refers to it – she was never into *monkey love*. That kind of love is not real, honest, nor unconditional in her eyes. It is only to appease and please but not to perform miracles. My parents needed a miracle for their daughter and that is exactly what they delivered. I am a miracle result of tough love.

Life's Source

> "Love is energy of life."
>
> *-Robert Browning*

Love is the source of life. Love is a healing energy. The entire Universe is made out of love. Love is a sacred vibrational language of the Universe. The Universe speaks to all its inhabitants and beings in the language of love. Fortunate are those who can speak this universal language. They are the enlightened. They are the awakened. They have woken up from the paralyzing hypnosis that the human race has been conditioned into. They have awakened to heaven on this Earth.

Love is everywhere around you. Love is life's oxygen. You need this oxygen. Without life's oxygen, you cannot thrive. Without love, you will suffocate. Without love, you can hardly survive. Without love you can only slowly die. You need love to heal and recover. You need love to realize the life of magic and abundance. You need love to exist. You might or might not be consciously aware but you cannot escape the truth. Love is all that you have been searching for your entire life.

You came here from love but then you were cut off from this vital energy. You were cut off from it through the system conditioning that does not want you to know true love. It does not want you to be connected to the most magnificent power there is. The establishment wants you weak because only weak individuals can be controlled and manipulated. Only weak and frail persons can be told how to think and how to be through organized beliefs, education, and politics. Only weak individuals can be turned into the system's slaves and become forever consumers who can never have enough. Only fragile individuals need to be saved by others. Only the weak depend on others.

The system does not want you to find the true source of love within you. The system wants you to depend on others for your life's energy. That is the only way that you can be manipulated. It is the only way that you can be starved. It is the only way to make you forever hungry.

Love is a transformation. It is a transformation from doing business into being love yourself. It is a migration from the known and familiar into something completely unknown. That is why love hurts so much. You are building a gate into bliss. Love hurts because it brings a revolution within you. Every revolution hurts because you have to leave the old for the new. The old is your comfort zone. It is the familiar that makes you feel safe and cozy. You are comfortable in the old. The new is scary. The new is not familiar. You cannot use the same mental instructions in this new place. You have to become someone completely different. You need to kill the old within you. It is your ego construct that will block you every time because in the new, you do not need ego. In the new, your mind is absolutely useless.

It reminds me when I made a decision to leave communist Czechoslovakia and move to the United States. Looking at it today, I was crazy. I knew no one. I had ten dollars in my pocket and one green suitcase. I spoke broken English. I had no cellphone or internet to be in touch with my family thousand miles away. *"You have lost your mind,"* many would tell me. They were absolutely right. I was not thinking and that was exactly the point. I lost my mind. Because I was not thinking I was not living in fear. My mind was not in my way. Because I was not limited by fear I was able to do anything. If it was today, some thirty years later, I do not think I would be able to do the same. My mind would be in my way, forcing me to consider all the necessary precautions and things that could go wrong. It would try to make all the necessary arrangements. The list would be a mile long. It would take forever to plan such a radical move. It would become impossible.

I was only nineteen when I immigrated. I did not have much of the fear-based programming too settled within me yet. I was young. I had a dream. I was willing to risk anything for my vision. I wanted to live the American dream so much that I was willing to die for it. I was willing to climb the mountains for it. I was willing to sacrifice the comfort of friends and family for a world filled with strangers.

This is the kind of dedication that distinguishes those who achieve their dreams from those who just dream. You need to want your vision so much that you are willing to die for it. You have to become your vision itself. You need to feel it down into your bones and every cell in your body. You cannot have any doubts. You have to trust in life and all there is. You have to have faith that no matter what, you will be always okay.

To reach your dreams, you have to lose your mind. You have to be crazy. You have to ignite the fire within you. You have to let it burn within you. It has to hurt for you to grow and be better. You have to embrace the pain and transformation because only that can make you rise higher.

Love is the only thing that is worth living for. For that you need to give love your total attention. You have to make love your absolute priority. You have to stop living for money and greed that are only driven by fear. When you fear, you cannot love. You need to start living for love. Start asking not only yourself but others what they do for love. Do not ask what they do for money. Money is just an illusion to keep you weak. Work for love as it is the most powerful force of the Universe. Everything else is secondary. If the things you are engaged in are for love then you have a real purpose. Anything that is not for love is merely a vehicle.

Love is your gateway to the stars. Love is your connection to God. Love is fire. Love is light. Love is your gateway to a heaven. Love is your answer.

Contract on Love

> "Love is a flower, you've got to let it grow."
>
> *-John Lennon*

Being in love is miraculous. The process itself is thrilling and enchanting. It's the most incredible feeling of joy and excitement. When you are in love, it seems like your entire world has transformed. You feel so good. You feel beautiful. You feel healthy. You feel lot of energy. You feel powerful. You feel like a super hero. Everything around you looks gorgeous and amazing. The colors look brighter. The sky is more beautiful. Food tastes more delicious. It is as if a magic veil has lifted and the world around you transformed. The truth is the external world did not change. What changed was your inner world. Your inner energy has increased dramatically and you rose higher. You intensified your electromagnetic field. When you are in love, your energy permeates and you radiate. You glow.

You spend most of your life living through your mind, however, which is running a program based on all kinds of fears. This results in majority of your energy being low. You become negative without being even consciously aware. When you are in love, however, you step out of this default set of negative instructions and start functioning through your heart. You rise higher. You rise in love. Functioning and living through your heart sets you free from your ego and your fears.

When you are in love you fear nothing. You are willing to go to the end of the world for love. You are ready to conquer the world. There are no barriers and you feel powerful. You become a champion who can do anything. That's what is so beautiful about being in love. Love gives you wings to fly. If you would connect your brain to EEG machine you will see how greatly increased your energy is. This is also what you emit to your external world. This is what other people instantly notice and it is usually very hard to hide, isn't it? Maybe you have been in a situation where two lovers were trying to suggest that they are just friends but you knew otherwise. It was due to their unique energy and vibration they were emitting. It was undeniable.

The reason for this is, when you are in love you fill your entire body with a warm and potent energy force. You vibrate on higher frequency. You feel complete and happy in that moment. You feel ecstatic. You are in a state of euphoria. It seems as all problems have magically disappeared and that everything becomes achievable. Like a miracle, all resistance dropped and you are just floating. You can go day and night making love. You do not need to sleep. You do not need to eat. You feel super human power.

This is your natural state of being. This is how you are when you are connected to your true self. This is who you are. This is how you feel when you are fully connected to your mind, body, and spirit. This is the divine feeling of being whole and complete. This is the feeling when you achieve your inner peace. This is Samadhi. It is this place we all are traveling towards. This is the dreamed destination of your existence, to be in love and feel the forever honeymoon through your every day experience.

We all are on the same journey. Some will get there sooner and some will get there later. Some will never get there. Everyone's journey is different. Everyone's pace is different but this is eventually where your spiritual teachers was it Jesus, Moses, Muhammad or Buddha were trying to take you to. This is the sacred place. They were not trying to take you to a different person, job, or political achievement. They were trying to bring you back to love.

Love is fluid energy within you and everywhere around you. Love is the vibration of the Universe. Love is all there is. Love is what connects you with everything else. Love is life's oxygen. Love is universal energy of this world. You cannot contain it. Love must flow. You cannot put limitations on it or secure it by any contracts. Love can never have any contracts in fact.

When you try to put borders around your love, you are building a prison not only for others but yourself as well. You are cutting yourself from the source of life. You are suffocating and slowly dying. Love is infinite. Love is freedom.

Love can never be secured. Love can never be protected by anything else. Love alone is your protection itself. You cannot limit or own love. You cannot make love a prison. Anyone imprisoned will spend their entire life either planning their escape or will get used to a dismal life in prison as it is with lifetime prisoners.

Whenever lifetime prisoners are released, they usually very quickly end up back in their prison. Prison is all they know. They got conditioned and accustomed to a structured life of misery. They have warm meals there. They have a place to sleep. They have a healthcare and people taking care of them. No matter how good or bad a life in prison looks to the outsider it is all these people know. They can only lean to the known because the known is their comfort zone. It is their security. They have a routine and it gives them a sense of safety. Being out there in the world on their own is scary. It is dangerous. They no longer know how to function on their own. They feel lost. It is unknown world so they rather return back the known prison than enjoy their newly gained freedom. They no longer know how to do it. They would have to change. They would have to become someone completely new and that is a painful process. For that, most of prisoners chose to die in the comfort of their secure cells.

Mikhail Naimy writes in his book named, The Book of Mirdad, *"Love is the only freedom from attachment. When you love you are attached to nothing. Manmade prisoner by the love of a woman and woman made prisoner by the love of a man are equally unfit for freedom's precious crown.*

But man and woman made as one by love, inseparable, indistinguishable are verily entitled to the prize."

Marriage as we know it today is an interesting institution. Those who are in want out and those who are out want in. Contracts and laws are for those who do not know how to love. It is for the ones who need to secure their highly priced possession and use a threat of a punishment if certain rules are not obeyed. Law and contracts are for those who are asleep. They are not consciously aware of themselves or their actions. They are not in touch with themselves.

Love is the sacred language of the Universe. It is the language of the heart. Contracts, laws and negotiations is a business language of the mind. It is the ego-driven mind that is calculating, manipulating and insecure. For that, it needs assurances and contracts that are then further enforced by steep punishments. It is relationship of force. This is not love.

Where are you going? Who are you going with? Why are you going there? What time will you be back? What are you wearing? This is not love nor freedom either. You have been conditioned into a mental prison. Attachment is the root of your pain. You associate your loved one with an ownership. This has been programmed into the human psychology for many generations. It is the trans-generational karma.

It has not always been like this. Humans first lived in tribes. Family as we know it today came only to existence to protect private property. When man realized that he does not need to roam the land but can claim land instead, it became his psychic revolution. People who had more property than the others became powerful. They wanted to ensure their wealth went only to their children. Their sense of property extended not only to things but also to people. This is known as the hundreds of years of slavery establishment. Man also made woman part of this property. It was not until this time that there was any other need than to come together in love and communion. It was greed manifesting as an ownership need that gave rise to our issues and state of separation.

The state and organized belief establishment is very much aware that once this founding "proprietorship" family structure is gone they will be gone too. They will naturally invest all their powers to ensure this does not happen. For that, you have great tax benefits to be married. You get deductions to have children and get applause by being a typical family. The establishment will continue to program the minds of generations to keep you in fear and away from discovering the source of life. It wants you in dark. It doesn't want you to awaken to your consciousness. For that, the establishment will continue to build your ego that will fight anything and anyone who will try to expose the truth.

You do feel, however, that things are falling apart. You are searching for truth because only truth can set you free. Only truth can liberate you and release you from a prison of your suffering. You were born free. You were born into love. It is your first-birth right. Millions of people continue to live locked with chains on their ankles. You are lifelessly dragging through life with chained balls attached to you. You do not think there is anything you can do. In reality, you just got used to your prison. The duvet of love is falling apart but at least there is someone with you in the bed to keep you company in your misery.

Love is not just encounter of male and female's hormones. It is also not a merger of business terms, financial benefits, or baby production scheme. Any of these kind of arrangements are not out of love but pure needs of self-realization and name continuation arising from fear.

There is only being together in love. Love is meeting of two awakened souls to share their love because they have already found it within themselves. They found their love and now they are sharing it with each other. None of them is needy to gain anything from the other person. There is no artificial force keeping them together. They are both free and through their individual freedom, they joined in love, peace, and harmony. Love must give you freedom. Love is a freedom. Love empowers you to rise higher. Love empowers you to keep going higher and higher. Love never keeps you chained or imprisoned. Only love can make you reach the sky.

Only love can give you wings to fly.

Chapter 7

FROM SEX TO AWAKENING

"Love is the absence of judgment."
-*Dalai Lama*

Unlike Animals

What's so special about humans? Most will say it's the size of our brain. We are also a species that created a language as a communication tool. Even though animals are not using any artificial language, they do communicate on a very profound level. They use vibration to communicate with each other as a sacred language. A language, which all beings share because the Universe does not speak English.

The Universe speaks in terms of vibrations. There are vibes we can feel but we are yet to fully tune ourselves to master this language like our animal friends. What is, however, the most captivating differentiator about humans, is our exaggerated lust for sex. This makes us quite the unique species in the entire animal kingdom.

Sex is on our mind at any given time. We think about it. We dream about it. We plan it. We prepare for it. We perform it. We evaluate it. Sex is on our brains unlike any other creature on this planet. To bring this into perspective, there are thousands of intercourses for every single birth. Even the few and truly monogamous animals are only having sex as the priest orders: to reproduce only, infrequently and very quietly.

Human beings utilize sex for anything from building friendship, providing pleasure, connecting to doing business. We also use sex to tie the knot, which most the time results in looking more like a joint venture, rather than a vow of unconditional love until death us apart.

Albert Einstein tried to console a female friend in a letter. She had learnt that her husband was having an affair. Einstein advised her to not take it personally by explaining to her that cheating was the norm among humans. *"I am sure you know that most men (as well as quite a number of women) are not monogamously endowed by nature."* wrote Albert Einstein.

"Nature will come through even stronger if convention and circumstances are putting resistances in the way of the individual. When a man forces himself to remain monogamous, it is a bitter fruit for everyone involved." explained Einstein to his friend, whose husband was unfaithful. He explained that people have a natural desire to have affairs, and it didn't do any good for them to resist the urge to do so.

We are having sex twenty-four-seven for every other cause than giving birth to a new life. Even the most sexually active and closest to us, the bonobos chimps, cannot beat us to the task. It is only us, humans, that engage in intercourse whenever we can think about it. With that, having sex without the purpose of conceiving a baby is more human than animalistic behavior. Having sex strictly to create a new life and only once in a blue moon is therefore more animalistic than human, unlike what we have been made to believe. A horny dog trying to hump every possible female in his proximity is acting more like a human rather than an animal. A partner that wants to have sex only a couple of times a year, is acting more like an animal that is in peace with himself rather than an unsettled human.

FROM SEX TO AWAKENING

Sex is promoted everywhere we look in our everyday life. Our entire society is built around it. Sex is the best tool how to lure a customer in. Sex means money. Sex sells and never fails to deliver. From sexy lingerie advertisements on TV, attractive human body billboards, literature, to lyrics in songs. You name it! Sex is on every corner you look, it is on everyone's mind.

Viagra sales break a record every year while over forty percent of American women suffer with sexual dysfunction according to the medical industry reports. Sex has become one of the most lucrative business industries. The corporate world quickly found a way to cash in on it. NBC news reported in 2015 that pornography is a ninety seven billion industry globally according to Kassia Wosick, assistant professor of sociology at New Mexico State University. Around ten percent of that comes from the United States.

The New York Times Magazine issued a cover story "Naked Capitalist: There's No Business Like Porn Business." Frank Rich, the author, writes that pornography is bigger than any of the major league sports and most likely bigger than Hollywood. Porn is "no longer a sideshow to the mainstream, it is the mainstream," Rich said.

The truth is, pornography has become a mainstream entertainment in our society. From billboards to viral videos online to social media sites. Social media sites like Twitter are becoming a paradise for pornography. It is home to an estimated ten million plus porn accounts. Pornographic content on this site has spread like a tornado. Analysis from Channel 4 News in 2015 concluded that one in every thousand tweets is pornographic. The truly devastating news is that Twitter naturally became a wonderland for child pornography as well. At the time of the survey, there was an estimated number of fourteen thousand active accounts involving children as young as five years old or below the age of fifteen.

There are close to twenty five million porn sites and three thousand dollars are spent every second on porn. Pornography search requests are made at a rate of sixty eight million each day. Over one hundred thousand searches are for child pornography per day. According to an infographic porn site Paint Bottle, porn takes up a huge percentage of Internet bandwidth. They claim thirty percent of all data transferred across the Internet is porn. YouPorn, one of the largest video porn sites, streams six times the bandwidth as Hulu. PornHub, the world's most popular porn site reported twenty eight billion total visits in 2017. That means that eighty one million a day, almost four million an hour and over fifty thousand people per minute are viewing porn.

Forty six percent of online viewers are married men and they aren't necessarily watching it during the evening, behind closed doors. Twenty percent of men and thirteen percent of women are watching porn from their corporate offices during their working hours. There is also a significant amount of children under the age of eighteen searching for porn.

One study reported that Americans spend more money at strip clubs than on Broadway, regional theaters, the opera, the ballet, jazz and classical music performances combined. "Life is short, have an affair" was a famous slogan used by Ashley Madison, a commercial website enabling extramarital affairs, that got hacked into in 2015. It was the "Impact Team" that stole and publicly released data of thirty-two million people who were cheating. CNN conducted a quick review where they found close to seven thousand addresses linked to people serving the American and Canadian governments. There were thousands of people serving the U.S. Army, Navy, Marines and Air Force violating Uniform Code of Military Justice. Adultery is a prosecutable offense that can lead to a year in confinement and dishonorable discharge. The data leak disclosed names, addresses and phone numbers of public figures, celebrities, politicians, priests, military members, public servants, high ranked executives among millions of regular citizens.

It would be very hard for anyone to deny that we have a sweet tooth for sex while traditional marriage seems to be under a great threat with over a fifty percent divorce rate. Even the people we worship and consider as role models such as our country leaders, presidents, religious figures, and many others; rolled in the mud due to their not so honorable family values exposed. There have been hundreds of priests confessing to hundreds of thousands of sexual crimes against children in the past two decades alone. The monetary awards in the U.S. Catholic abuse crisis now total over three billion dollars. There have been over a hundred thousand victims and some of these numbers include children under the age of ten years old.

According to the U.S. State Department there are half a million humans trafficked every year. Eighty percent of these cases involve sexual exploitation. Eighty percent of these cases are female and half are children. Human trafficking is the third largest international crime behind drugs and arms trafficking. It is estimated to generate a profit of thirty two billion dollars every year. Half of that amount is made in industrialized countries.

In the United States, about twenty million women or eighteen percent have been raped during their lifetime. Only sixteen percent of those women reported the incident to authorities. In 2006 alone, three hundred thousand college women were raped. In 2012, there were close to sixty three thousand cases of child sexual abuse reported. According to the Bureau of Justice Statistics National Criminal Victimization Survey from 2012, there were over three hundred and forty six thousand reported cases of sexual assaults on people twelve years or older.

Desire

> "A body is just a body. It is our desires that make it into something else."
>
> -L. E. Bowman

It is obvious; there is a great discrepancy between public façade and our true values. Demand creates supply and that's exactly what calls for a great business. Sex has become one of the best moneymaking machines thriving on the sexual chaos humanity found itself in.

Humanity as whole has not only shut its eyes on sexual energy but turned it into a war. The results are devastating. Ninety eight percent of man's mental illness and ninety nine percent of woman's hysteria is due to the suppression of this energy. People are aggressive, unhappy and suffering.

If there were aliens to visit our society and looked at our magazines, billboards, paintings, photographs, books, music, TV programs, movies and poetry they would be astonished. They would be astonished that the existence of the human kind is centered around sex. They would be even more astonished after talking to a man whose mind is filled with sex, yet he never talks about it. He would talk about politics, sports and God but would mention nothing about sex. There would be not a single word about it although that's what his mind is filled with and his entire world around him. He would pretend like sex does not exist.

Our society corrupts the mind by building a body, pure and divine temple, into a sexual tool. It is done through sex-fused ideology and provocative images to make the mind desire, to make the mind want. It has turned humans perverted. At the same time the society has brainwashed the mind with sex-suppressive propaganda of morals, religious and family values built on crumbling foundation. It is a recipe for a disaster. It is exactly where we are finding ourselves today - disastrous state of confusion and insanity. There is a boiling war within us and it reflects on the world around us. A world based on ego driven, masculine mind that has been corrupted. A mind that has been turned against life.

Life force, however, is much greater energy. It will always prevail no matter how hard the mind tries. That is the disconnect we can feel. That is the crumbling world we wonder about. It is all connected. The search is on. It can no longer be disputed. The sexual energy in humans is greater than any power. It is greater than electricity. It is greater than nuclear energy. We saw what a small atom of matter did in Chernobyl and Hiroshima. We have also seen what an atom of human energy can produce. It gives a birth to a new life. It creates a new person. That person can be Jesus, Gandhi, Buddha or you. A tiny small atom of human energy carries a legend like Abraham, Moses or Muhammad within itself. What a miracle.

We have to find a new way out of this craziness we have been seduced to. We have to present humanity a new way. We have to open a new gateway, otherwise we will continue to run in the same vicious circle and destroy ourselves. The concept of sex that has been in existence so far has not enabled humans to open any new gateway other than sex. When there is no new entrance this sacred energy gets trapped and drives a person insane. This person now has trapped nuclear energy and becomes a ticking bomb. It needs a release. It is a forceful energy of life that now turns destructive and destroys all in its reach. Instead of creating life it turns against life. It turns into a weapon.

There seems to be something horribly wrong with what has been stamped into our blood lineage about sex, relationships, and official mating arrangements. If things were set in its true and natural way, there would be no pornography, prostitution, divorce, cheating or sexual abuse. Something is horribly wrong with us.

It is time to evolve our thinking and approach to life in general. Life is one of the most beautiful and precious gift we could have been gifted with. Just the matter that we have the ability to live in this new day is a miracle. Life is such a blessing, yet humans have turned it into such a suffering and pain. We can have a completely different world available to us if we decide to take a critical look and examine why this is all happening to us. Why did life turn into such a struggle? Why do things lose its spark so quickly? Why is there so much dishonesty, preying on each other and cheating?

We need to break out of the mental enslavement that we have been programmed into. The first step towards freedom is accepting the truth, even though it might not be convenient. Accepting the truth is a must in order to create a better world for our children and their children. We cannot afford to fear it any longer. Truth hurts because it causes change. This change refers to a new reality that will allow you to evolve. Embrace it and look towards the new stage in your life. Only an incomplete and disturbed individual will use another person's body for his own pleasure and satisfaction. This will only happen when you are disconnected from unconditional love, your natural state of being.

You turned love into a business and you feel you are about to go bankrupt at any given moment. You need more attention. You need more passion. You need more admiration. You need more assurance. You turned love into a self-validation, self-gratification and self-assurance tool. You turned your love into an obsession. You turned your love into an ownership. You need more and more because you fell into a black hole of emptiness. It is dark, empty, and cold down there. You are shivering and you want heat. You know that only love can bring that warmth. But you do not know where to get true unconditional love and make it stay for an eternity. No one has ever showed unconditional love to you. This lack of unconditional love is why we are lost. The whole humanity fell into this dark freezing hole.

The human kind blocked their natural energy from within and removed themselves from the most powerful healing powers of the Universe. Humanity got off the grid and connected to the low dark energy of their ego. They are driven by politics and greed. For that, the human kind finds itself on a deserted island headed towards a disaster.

It is a scary deserted place where it is extremely lonely, and for that we need to use others. We exploit not only our own kind but other innocent beings such as children and animals to the fullest extent. Because of this disconnect from unconditional love, we have no true compassion for others. We forgot how to love ourselves and for that, we cannot truly love others. We can never give what we do not have.

We are searching for the spark and romance. We are searching for unconditional love and we cannot find it. Sex and personal relationships became an escape. It became an addiction, which like any addictions, is a very scary bond that your mind will not allow you to break. It is your ego at its highest ruling. Sex becomes your ego's addiction for self-validation and self-gratification. You need to unleash the nuclear energy that is boiling within you. There is a nuclear war broiling within you and sex is the only outlet. This outlet is the only time you can connect with the depths of your existence. It is in this depth where you can just be, and sex is the only tool you know how to reach there.

This is all happening because we turned sex into a dirty taboo and because we do not educate about its true divine purpose. We turned it into such a suffering and life itself along with it. Yet… sex is beautiful, playful, and joyous. It is a sacred energy exchange through communion in unconditional love. It is an incredible experience and amazing gift of a higher purpose if we only learn more about it. It was and will be here as long as life exists on this planet. You can turn your head away and get mad about it. You can deny it, but this is the truth. The entire planet is based on sex whether you like it or not. It is the bee collecting the pollen to fertilize the flower. It is the male bird parading in front of the female in order to mate.

Our entire life is involved in sex for its divine purpose. This entire Universe depends on sex for giving birth to life and yet, somehow, we got tricked into believing that this godly process is some kind of a sin. We have been made to believe that sex is something inappropriate that should never be discussed or acknowledged. This is where our problem lies. We turned our back on this nuclear force of the Universe. We blocked the energy of life and now it is trapped. It is like a ticking bomb to explode.

Sex Starvation

> "The decisive moment in human evolution is perpetual. That is why the revolutionary spiritual movements that declare all former things worthless are in the right, for nothing has yet happened."
>
> *-Franz Kafka*

Our mental maturity and true spiritual evolution is trapped in the ticking bomb of trapped sexual energy. It is at puberty where human maturity is trapped. Why puberty? At this age, sex matures in an individual and the society does not want you to evolve beyond that point. The system wants you sexually starved because a starved individual can be easily manipulated.

There is a nuclear energy boiling within and you are completely unaware. This sexual starvation is even worse than depriving a person of their sleep. Even the toughest man will become like a little puppy, following his master around when he doesn't get the much needed sleep. That is why sleep deprivation is one of the best methods to break an individual. It has been used by military and others for centuries. Sex is used for the same manipulation.

You can manipulate the sex and spiritually starved individual through greed, beliefs, or morals. You can use money as a carrot and he will spend the rest of his life chasing his tail thinking, money is his newly found God. Naturally, money can never fulfill him and for that, sex will continue to chase him. Or, you make him race after status and power. He will turn into a great politician and be convinced that it is his newly found God. Again, the love of power cannot fulfill him either and as a result, sex will continue to chase him.

There are one thousand and one ways on how the system can use this trapped nuclear force to maneuver and manipulate you. The society took your urge and gave you a pacifier. You keep sucking and sucking, thinking milk will come. That day never comes. How cruel! How inhumane! Sex has become a tool of torture for humanity, to keep you weak, corrupt, and starved. It has become a weapon of mass destruction being served right underneath our nose.

The prehistoric times show that homo-sapiens lived in communal arrangements. These type of practices can still be seen in certain areas of China, Africa to exotic Amazon. Some might consider those tribes primitive but before we jump into labeling and judging, let's examine it from an unbiased position please. Let's take for example, the Mosuo tribal community of Tibetan Buddhists in South West China. Their way of living is surprisingly modern.

Women are treated as equal to men and both genders have as many or as a few sexual partners as they like, free from judgment. Extended families raise the children and care for the elderly. They share their feelings and care for each other. There is a great level of harmony and peace among the community. There is no pornography, peeking at children's genitals, child abuse, sexual abuse, rape or anything of such kind that is so frequently seen in our *'civilized and emancipated'* communities. All the women help breastfeed other children and children have more than one father, because women practice sex with different men prior to conception and thereafter. It is done in this way to eliminate any parental fear or competition. All the children belong to all the men and women.

This culture views it as a highly beneficial attribute for the offspring. These children will always be loved, protected, and well cared by everyone. Every child is everyone's offspring. Because of that, no one would ever think to harm or endanger any of them. Those children never feel out of place and have a close connection with everyone within the community. This results in harmony and peace among everyone, as they all feel they are a part of everyone's family. There is no rivalry, jealousy nor murders unlike it is in the western modern cultures.

Marriage is not the goal in these cultures. The only reason for men and women to have a relationship of any sort is because of love and enjoyment for each other's company. If it runs its course, they quietly move on. There is no divorce and its ugly consequences turning love into hate, which can have such dramatic outcomes for innocent children dragged through the dirty laundry of their immature parents. The typical reason to stay together for the sake of children, social or financial needs does not apply there either. It is that simple. Life is that simple, until we complicate it. One has to wonder if these naturally emancipated residents of 'primitive' cultures could show the western civilized world a different approach to family life? You be the critic.

There are many wars we, as a society, are engaged in. It's the war against hunger or cancer. It's the war against terrorism or drugs. The greatest of all wars, however, is the war on sex, which we have entangled ourselves in. We do not speak about it nor are we aware of this war. It acts like a leaking gas, you cannot see it or touch it, but you can smell that something is terribly wrong. Things are breached and they need to be fixed. We somehow evolved into a species of conflict and fight. We are the only species in constant war.

The more we are fighting, the more there is something to fight about. Is it possibly that we need to stop fighting all together? Is it possibly because we avoid conflict by not speaking the truth in order to keep peace, we actually create a war inside of us? In order to create a different world, we must evolve. We must evolve from a state of conflict into a state of full understanding and inner peace. We must evolve from sex to higher consciousness.

This is the time to understand the two-sole purpose of sex. The first purpose is clear and obvious. It was given to us to bring a new life in to this world. It is a miracle that a new being can be created from one tiny cell. A cell that was formed by the union of a male and female sex cell. This tiny little cell carries the genetic material, the DNA or the blueprint of a new being that will be further formed and shaped by the given environment he/she is being planted in. What an amazingly miracle of life.

The second purpose of sex is almost the same or even of higher importance. It is our missing link towards our evolution and awakening. We have now been searching for thousands of years, for the depth of our being that we cannot attain from a normal life. That's what all the rush and panic is about. During our normal life, we have all kinds of experiences. We go shopping, we go to a movie theater or a restaurant. We go to work or the local store. None of these experiences, however, take us deep into our being as our sexual experience.

There is nothing like having a sexual intercourse, where two extremely important things happen in the deep depths of our being. First, the mind quiets down and it becomes completely silent. There is no ego and with no ego there is no time. In a moment of orgasm, there is an ecstasy where the ego and its social roles disappear. You are no longer a father or a mother. You don't worry about your job. You don't worry about the taxes or the bills. When you have an orgasm, there is no time to worry. You ascend your mind. You go beyond time. There is no past, present or future. Time completely disappears during sexual experience. You are in a moment of complete interconnection. All your problems dissolve in an instant and you feel free. No one is judging nor competing with you. It is just *you* in your purest and most perfect way possible. You feel liberated and unrestricted. You love this feeling of eternal bliss because there is no pressure or stress. Even though, it's a brief moment, the experience feels divine. What you have experienced is a connection to your highest state of consciousness. You have experienced your spirit and your infinite powers.

These infinite powers go beyond your body and your physical form. You felt divine, as if God was within you. For a moment, you got a taste of awakening and enlightenment. You have experienced a state of Samadhi, when God is within you. A God that can heal and create a new life. A God that can make miracles happen.

You want to experience these feelings as many times as possible. You want to bask in it every moment. You want to have that feeling of bliss all the time. It is what you have been searching for your entire life. But you cannot live in that sexual moment forever. In search of that blissful state, you have been engaging in sex for many years. You have been looking and searching. You have tried different partners, situations and positions because you know it is somewhere there, but somehow you can not quite keep it. You can not make it stay. It is because you do not know how to use the sacred tool of sex to rise higher and touch the sky. No one has ever taught you that sex is your door to spirituality and your connection to the entire Universe.

There is a spiritual teaching within sex that we have been denying as a society. In order to evolve into a higher intelligence we need to learn about this spiritual experience. Sex is the gateway to our higher consciousness. If we cannot be aware of that experience and the missing link, we cannot rise above sex. In sex, we will continue to exist and we will continue to die as inadequate, incomplete beings. You can only liberate yourself from sex and its addiction when you start having spiritual experience where mind completely dissolves. It is Samadhi. It is a final stage where orgasmic union with the divine is reached without sex. On this day, you become finally free.

Chapter 8

STATE OF SEPARATION

> "No one is born hating another person because of the color of his skin, or his background, or his religion. People must learn to hate, and if they can learn to hate, they can be taught to love, for love, comes more naturally to the human heart than the opposite."
>
> *- Nelson Mandela*

Fear Programming

One of the best days ever was when I stopped watching TV. I never realized how toxic and negative the news are until I actually stopped watching it. It is constantly feeding you fear either in direct or indirect way. It is no accident that it is called programming. It is directly programing your mind with fear. The direct way is obvious. It is all the negative news who killed who, what plane crashed where and which country will be first to drop a nuclear bomb on you. It never ends and it is only getting worse. We have created a world of war and conflict because we as species are at war within ourselves.

Our outer world only mirrors what our inner world is. Then you look up to the authorities to bring peace not realizing they want us fighting and divided. They do not want you connected to love, your natural state of being. They don't want you to know the power of love. They want you to know only fear because they want you weak and powerless. It is very beneficial to the system to keep us apart and pretend they are the Salvation Army coming to save a day. What an illusion.

The indirect way of fear is all the things the media tells you that you need. All the things you cannot live without. They are programming you who you need to be. It creates a feeling of a need and builds a state of lack down in your subconscious, your brain hard drive. It becomes a part of your computer program, playing the same set of instructions repeatedly without you even realizing that something might be wrong. Your two-car garage is filled to the roof with gadgets, bikes, treadmills and all kinds of things. Your closet is packed with clothes and you have shoes to dress an entire ballroom of people.

While your life is filled with material things you do not have enough. Only if you can get this latest electronic, BBQ grill or self-navigating car you will find your forever happiness. If you buy this latest make up you will be the most beautiful girl. All this makes you feel incomplete and in constant need to become someone else. It creates a state of lack and emptiness. It is the perfect strategy to build a consumer who has never enough – there will be always new tricks and new gadgets to sell you. The economy must produce more and more.

Every year the corporate growth numbers get higher and higher. Sales grew thirty percent last year so the push is to exceed it this year to fifty percent. The following year it should be seventy percent. Year after year, you must produce and create more. It never ends. We need higher profits and bigger piles of money. You are the money machine. It might cost you your health, your marriage, your planet or your sanity but the system does not care. You are just a little part of the entire money making machine and this machine is hungry, very hungry. It will consume you if you do not wake up. It is modern times slavery.

Constantly building up for the future that never comes and then you die. This feeds the ego. The ego structure has never enough. The lacking, the needing will forever keep you in a state of separation because you are looking on the outside to fill yourself with things, people and experiences. The more you accumulate more empty you feel. You live in hopes of the next greatest thing to complete and satisfy you. The issues is that happiness never comes externally.

Happiness is an inside job. There are so many poor people in the world. All they have is their money. *"Money is not everything,"* is the saying but how could this possibly be? If you have billions of dollars you can buy anything and be anywhere. The truth is that all you are buying is an escape ticket from yourself. You are at war inside of you and need a constant distraction and entertainment to keep yourself busy and entertained. You hate the idea of boredom and loneliness. The issue is, however, as you keep maturing and experiencing all the joy of wealth, you realize that the riches is elsewhere.

You suffer because you desire. You want a bigger house and more expensive car. You want more respect, more attention, more happiness, more adventure, more sex. You want and want. Your desires are ceaseless. Your perpetual desire creates a state of lack, not having nor being enough. Not being complete. The system wants you like this. The system wants you incomplete, insane and miserable. It is the only way how you can be controlled and manipulated.

Pleasing Others

> "The most difficult thing in
> life is to know yourself."
>
> -Thales

Years of programming of my false self did a great job in building my ego. My ego took ownership of my existence and turned me into a snob. There was a chip on my shoulder for as long as I can remember. It was not intentional but a result of the process of becoming. It was the other self that had to comply and conform. It had to fit in with others. I had such a hard time doing that. It was against my own beliefs. I had to do it, however, in order to be accepted. I had to comply with the conditioned programming of the society. I felt like I was living the life of another person. I could not recognize myself. I felt torn apart on the inside. Lost in this frenzy, I did not know who I am and became confused. I was living someone else's life which became all about pleasing others. In my attempt to please others, I lost my own identity.

First, it was my parents. I always needed to make them proud by complying with the rules of society. I had to be good at school by earning exceptional grades. I had to be polite. I had to be respectful to authority. It felt unnatural. I felt forced. It felt like I was being molded into some kind of form that was not fitting me. The mold was too small. I felt unimaginably contained. I felt squished. I did not want to be a part of this complacent person formed by someone else's idea of perfection.

I wanted to be me. I wanted to be a person with all her beautiful imperfections. I wanted to be a being that did not have to live in fear. I did not want to live under a microscopic scrutiny. I did not want to live in fear of judgment. I simply wanted to know that it is okay to trip and fall. If I do fall, I wanted someone to be there for support. I wanted to know that someone would help me stand up without labeling me 'bad' for life. I knew that I make mistakes and I only wished to own them in order to learn and grow.

I did not want to fear being judged and wrongfully labeled by merely being a human. I did not want to live like a robot of perfection. I did not want to fear that a mistake can possibly write me off for good. I was living in fear. I was living in a false perception that wanted to please everyone. I had to please my parents. I had to please my teachers by being a good student. I had to please the authorities by being a law abiding citizen. I even had to please my friends. My own family was no exception; I had to please my husband and my children.

At work, I had to please the boss, my colleagues and I had to please the customers. The entire world expected to be pleased by me. It created such a tension and anxiety within me. I spent my precious days in constant calculations. I was constantly evaluating everything. I started to continually second guess myself, which created a state of self-doubt. I was fueling my mind and my false self by wondering if I had done the right thing.

I was wondering if I had said things correctly. I wondered if I could have done things differently. I was playing different scenarios in my mind because there was always a way to do things better. This was only because I was not conscious. I was not mindful. I was run by a subconscious programming of the mind. I was filled with regret, fear and doubt. I felt an immense pressure on how to accomplish perfection at all times. I was wondering how I can possibly continue doing it for the rest of my life. I was going insane. I realized that by not speaking my truth and avoiding conflict I was creating a war within me.

I realized that I am enough when I decided I can no longer live a life of pretending. I simply wanted to be authentic. I wanted to be me. I wanted to be free from the responsibility of pleasing others. I just wanted to speak my truth. I no longer wanted to feed others sweet, paralyzing lies. I needed to wake up from my nightmare. I needed to wake up from the chronic psychosis the entire world has been seduced to. I realized that I do not need the approval of others to be worthy. This is my life and mine alone. Only I can walk my path. This journey is to be walked by me, alone. No one else can walk in my shoes. No one else can make me happy. No one else is there to save me, I have to save myself. I realized I have to become my own hero and so I did. It was just like that. All I had to do was give myself the permission and the power to do it.

Happiness is unbelievable. It is hard to believe that a person can actually be happy. It normally seems exactly the opposite. It is much more believable to talk about a person's disease, sorrow and depression. People will believe that. It seems perfectly fine and normal. It sounds natural. No one will question it. Sigmund Freud was a famous Austrian neurologist who spent forty years studying the human mind. He worked with thousands of people and studied thousands of disturbed minds. He came to a conclusion that *happiness* is a fiction. People only know how to be unhappy. They do not know how to be happy. Only the human kind is unhappy. Have you noticed? Have you ever seen an unhappy tree? Have you ever seen an unhappy bird? Have you ever seen an unhappy flower? The entire nature around us is happy. The entire Universe conspires for each creation's happiness. Happiness is a natural state of being.

You can become very happy, ecstatically happy. You can become happier than any tree, bird, or flower. The reason for that is you can become fully aware of your happiness. The tree, bird, or flower cannot. They do not know how to attain that awareness. They know only how to be happy. They do not have any other choice. You, on the other hand, have a choice. You have a choice to be extremely happy or extremely unhappy.

Happiness is completely up to you. You have the complete freedom to decide how you want to be. This freedom, however, is very dangerous. It brings tremendous responsibility because you are now made fully responsible. It is you, who is in full charge.

You need nothing to be happy. You only need something to be unhappy about. Happiness is your natural state. Happiness is all there is. In order to be happy you need to surrender to what is. You need to let go of fear. You need to let go of your worry. You need to let go of judgment. Letting go of all these things will bring a major relief. It will bring a major shift into your life. It will deliver freedom that will rejuvenate your entire body. You will be finally able to breathe. You will be finally able to break from the mold of others. A mold that no longer fits you because it is too tight. A mold that is not truly you. Your wings will be ready, You will be ready to unleash the supernatural.

Extreme happiness happens when you align yourself with life. You are no longer someone fake but you are real. You put your mask down. You accept your faults, mistakes, and miss-steps. You forgive yourself. You align with the great good within you. You align with love. You are no longer in resistance of *what is*. Now, you harmoniously flow with anything you are doing. Any of your activities become a joy. You might be washing dishes and you find joy in it. You find it as a blessing that you have a place to stay and food to eat. For that, washing dishes becomes an activity of gratitude. It becomes joy. You might have a job as a waitress, bringing food to your customers. In that activity, you will see the blessing that you can walk. You will see the blessing that someone is employing you. You will see a blessing when your customer gives you a tip. You will see a blessing that you can be of a great service to someone. It is no longer a hardship or chore but a level of deep gratitude.

No matter what job you are performing, whether it's being a waitress, an engineer or a CEO you become deeply aligned with your activity. You will be gracious in the present moment. You will turn all those activities into a meditation. You will be fully aligned and equipped with the ability to find blessings. You will turn your regular activity into an activity of love. You will turn your activity or job into a privilege. When your activity becomes what you love to do, you will never work a single day in your life. Your days will transform from days of mere duties and chores into days of blessings and amazing opportunities. In this state, nothing can distract you and nothing can take your peace away. You will become peace itself.

Extreme happiness is a route to a life of joy. It is a life of everlasting honeymoon, which starts from the inside. Joy has nothing to do with the outer world. It is not caused by anything. Joy is spontaneous. It is a river of your own energy. If your energy is trapped, you cannot feel joy. You are no longer a river but a pond, where there is no flow. The water is murky and it smells. Fish or vegetation cannot live there because there is no flow of fresh water. There is no oxygen, and the water builds algae. There is no life in the pond. It is a pond of death.

River means life because water in the river is constantly flowing. There is plenty of fish and incredible vegetation in the river. It is fluid and alive. When you become that river, you feel alive. When you become a flowing river, you get only stronger. You become bigger and powerful. You collect additional creeks on your way and allow more flow to join you. You become a raging force that is traveling towards the ocean. You are headed towards the majestic force of wholeness. You feel the infinite movement within you. You feel lust for life. You live in joy and happiness for no reason.

Living in joy is ecstatic because it surpasses the founding law of cause and effect. You no longer need any *cause* to feel happy. It just happens for no specific reason at all. It surprises you. It takes your breath away. You leave the earth and reach the sky, where you become a shining star. This is what joy feels like. Buddha refers to joy as a continuum because it has no beginning or end. It is an eternal flow and an eternal continuity.

When you are a pond, you are slowly dying. You try to bring all kinds of tricks to your pond in order to keep it alive. You are trying to balance the potential hydration of your water. You have to clean the water. The pond needs to be constantly watched to keep it alive. Being a pond is a tiring job, it is a foolish job. It is something you are forced to do. The moment you forget to do it, you are back to dying. It is a dead end because a pond can never become a river. A pond will only be a pond; it can never turn into an ocean. Being a pond has no higher potential. Being a pond is being stagnant. There is no flow of energy in a pond. Do not settle to be a pond. You were destined to be a raging river that is destined to become an endless ocean.

There are so many people living the life of a stagnant pond. There is no inner flow so they try to bring it from the outside. They hope the outer riches will turn them into an ocean of abundance. They think that little bit more technology and science can make them rich. The rich man senses this more than the poor man. The poor man only sees darkness. He sees inner and outer darkness. He has no comparisons. A poor man has no reference. However, the rich man gets a glimpse of light through his temporary excitements. He buys a new boat and gets excited. He gets a hot girlfriend and gets excited. He keeps accumulating people and things but it does not bring the aspired enlightenment. The rich man is still living a life of a stagnant pond. The only difference is that his pond is very crowded. It is so crowded that there is no room to move. He feels more stuck than the poor man.

I know a very wealthy couple. They own many houses. Their driveway looks more like a luxury car dealership. They buy designer cloths and travel to exotic places for their vacations. They have plenty of money to last them and their children several lifetimes. Yet, they do not know how to truly enjoy life and all of its blessings. They continue to work endless hours at jobs they hate and stress every day over little details. They look for the cheapest deals they can get to make their dollar stretch to the maximum. They never have enough money or possessions. They feel their poverty. They are stressed over the things they have. They do not own things but are owned by things. Their marriage looks more like a misery. He cheated on her, so she cheated on him. Even though, it happened years ago, they can never forget or forgive. They have three children that are strangers to them. They know nothing about them beyond the college they attend, what car they drive and who they are currently dating. They are staying together because they need to keep each other company in their mutual misery. They are living in stale waters, where no energy flows.

Chose life in joy. Chose to be a beautiful flow of energy. Chose to be an ocean of endless possibilities. Chose happiness without being possessive or obsessive. Learn how to enjoy the world with all its beautiful blessings. Do not posses. Appreciate instead. Appreciate all that is being offered to you into its full capacity without being greedy. Enjoy nice things without clinging to them or making them a necessity of your happiness. Enjoy the sun, the vast blue sky. Enjoy the blooming flowers and the afternoon breeze. It is all there for your enjoyment.

STATE OF SEPARATION

Do not ever try to own. You came here empty handed and you will also leave empty handed. Learn how to be a master of your existence by enjoying the journey. Don't be obsessed with the destination. Life is an exciting play, which should be played with all your intentions and with all you got. Do not stress over winning or losing in your play.

Life is not about winning or losing but how much you *enjoyed* the game. This is the true spirit of playing. To master your game, you have to first master yourself. Once you master yourself, your entire life will be such a joy.

There will be people on your journey that might leave your life because they cannot take your transformation. They might leave because they were not able to handle the new you. They cannot handle your newly gained freedom. They will not be able to take your truth. Some people will be threatened by your power and freedom. Some people will hate that you changed. It is quite alright, this is nothing for you to worry about. These people are only reflection of who they are. What they think is their personal business; it is nothing of your concern. All you have to remember is that people who love, will love. People who hate, will hate. It has nothing to do with you. You are no longer coming from fear and for that you can only love. You love because it not only feels amazing but it is also extremely healthy for you.

You know who you are and you know that you love. Because you love, you can only speak the truth. As long as you are coming from love, there is nothing to regret or fear. Love is the most enduring power of this Universe. Love will always prevail no matter what. By stepping out of fear into love, you will release your pain and trauma. You will release the dark energy within you that has been building up to a disease. Through this release, you will allow a new energy to come in. You will allow health and healing to enter your life. You will allow prosperity to enter. You will allow a world of abundance to open up to you. You will allow a powerful force of life to enter.

All you have to do is, decide. All you have to do is to ask and you shall be given.

Today is your day!

Addiction

> *"Every saint has a past and every sinner has a future."*
>
> -Oscar Wilde

Addiction is a favorite past time of humans. There are all kinds of addictions. The only difference between them is that our society recognizes only a few as a problem. The ones that are illegal are those that the society does not financially benefit from. Any other addictions are perfectly fine and even encouraged by the educational, law enforcement, medical and political establishment. It is only those addicted to illegal drugs and alcohol that get special attention for being criminals. We point our fingers at them and label them as *"bad"* people. These people do have a problem but the fact remains that most people have the same problem – only they go about it in a different way than is approved by the system for financial gains.

Some people are addicted to food. I used to be one of them. My life was all about food. It was constantly on my mind. What am I having for lunch? Where am I going for dinner? What kind of desert will I make over the weekend? I even invented an excuse that I need to eat every two hours because my blood sugar level was low. I told myself I would faint if I did not eat. You can say that food was my big love affair, as it is for so many others. I was eating because I was happy. I was eating because I was sad. I was eating because I was bored. I was eating because the food was there. I was eating because it was time to eat. I was constantly stuffing something into my mouth because I was not conscious of it at all.

Coffee was one of my biggest addictions. I could not function without it. I could not get up in the morning without being stimulated by a strong cup of Turkish coffee. My other addiction was shopping. I was addicted to nice things. I had to have the latest shoes, the latest fashion, just the latest of everything. I used to decorate my existence like a Christmas tree. There was always some kind of new ornaments and decorations to improve my image. My ego loved it and the drive to do so only grew stronger with time. My need to shop was endless. It filled up my closet and not just that but my shopping treasures spread throughout the rest of our house like a cancer. My stuff was everywhere and still, it was never enough.

I was also a drug addict. The only difference was that the drugs I was addicted to were made legal. My kitchen cupboard looked more like a private pharmacy. You could find anything from Advil, Amoxicillin, and Celebrex to Prozac. I was not only addicted to these drugs but to my diseases as well. I was a professional patient. I was on a constant hunt for new things that could be wrong with me and what kind of new drug I could get in order to treat those diseases. The tragic part was that no one could see my addiction as an issue; furthermore, my legalized drug dealers only encouraged me in my self-destructive behavior. You cannot blame the doctors, though, because like any other businessmen, they had a business to run to make a living in order to support their family and their own addictions.

I had so many inner issues. It just happened that either they were made legal or no one knew about them. I was so perfectly wrapped in socially accepted morals and was an image of a perfect citizen while a war was being waged inside of me. I was a criminal of my own soul. I was insulting myself. I made life all about my family, my needs and myself. Life was all about me. I was a hamster in a wheel running to nowhere. I needed to keep myself entertained so I would not have to deal with my problems.

I did know, however, that one day, I would have to clean up my act and find peace. I knew that I could not keep running around and escaping myself forever. I knew that this is not how life was supposed to be. I knew that I will have to find a way toward my super consciousness that could finally guide me to the person I could be. A person of dignity and true values. A person who does not have to pretend or hide from anything nor anyone. A person who can be herself. A person who can finally be free. I knew that this version of me was there somewhere. I just had to take the journey to go find her.

People have so many different types of addiction – ranging from food, gambling, sex, pornography, shopping, alcohol and drugs to social media. We are species of addiction because we have not reached inner peace. Our minds are running at hundred miles per hour and we cannot turn it off. We are looking for an outlet. We are disconnected from ourselves. We do not know who we are. For that reason, we are always looking for an escape. It is only an escape from the self and the wrong beliefs of others. Your heart knows better. It is the pressure inside the head that is unbearable. We do not know what to do with ourselves. We have become the species of the lost.

Suicide

> "When you arise in the morning, think of what a precious privilege it is to be alive - to breathe, to think, to enjoy, to love."
>
> *-Marcus Aurelius*

Everyone is attempting suicide. There are only a few people that are not. These fortunate ones have realized that the life they have been gifted with is such a blessing. They have awakened to the realization of what an amazing gift they have received in the form of life. They see life's ups and downs as part of their journey. They are living life as if it was an adventure where every day brings something new and exciting.

They have learned how to see the good in everything. They have learned how to trust in life. They have learned how to trust people in general. They have learned to silence their minds. They have learned to live in the now. They have learned how to take things as they are. They have learned how not to judge. They have learned how to see their problems only as challenges that will help them improve and become better. They are the ones who have learned how to see every person that crosses their path as a holy encounter no matter what they bring with them. These people have learned how to truly live. These people are the blessed ones. These are the people who have unleashed their supernatural potential.

Then there are the rest who are busy attempting two types of suicides. The first is a slow suicide. I was also once a part of that group. I was attempting a slow suicide. I was killing myself for jobs that would replace me in a matter of days. I was killing myself to buy things that I did not need. I was killing myself to be someone I was not. There was so much of killing in my life that I even started to think about actually doing it. I was lost. I was desperate. Life was very hard. Despite the short moments of happiness, any feeling of true contentment was temporary. My happiness was dependent on the outer world. People and situations had power over me. It was up to their discretion how I felt in my inner world. It was a struggle. I was a puppet on a string.

I was living most of my days just to make it through. There were only a few exciting days here and there. I was *"just"* working, taking care of the kids and my family. I was 'making a living' as we say. There was no level of gratitude in any of that, however. There was no appreciation that I woke up and could breathe. There was no appreciation that I woke up and could walk. There was no appreciation that I had a safe home for my children and myself to sleep in. There was no gratitude that I had food on my table. There was no gratitude that I had a job and opportunity to provide for all that I have. There was no gratitude because I was living in a state of lack.

Now, living in a state of lack is like living in a hole. It is dark and empty in there. I had to always have something to look forward to – like an exotic vacation, a new car, food or sexual pleasure. My senses had to be constantly stimulated. I needed to be constantly pleased and satisfied. The moment I was not pleased I would get depressed. Life would suddenly turn dark again and throw me back into my hole. I was an addict of external things and people that made me feel validated, worthy and needed. I was needy.

No matter of how much I would bring into my life, I could never see it. My hole was filled to the roof with things, people and experiences; yet I could not see any of that. It was just me and my darkness. I was asleep in a deep, dark hypnosis of the matrix.

Then one day, I was finally dying. I was in an emergency room fighting for my life and I suddenly realized how much I wanted to live. I looked back at my life and saw all that I have. I looked back and realized how blessed I have been. I had to die before I actually died in order to understand the secret to life. I visited the other side to see what it is all about. I had a near death experience that only assured me that there is absolutely nothing to fear.

Even death is not the end. We are an endless energy manifesting itself as humans so we can know how wine and cheese tastes like. Despite my acts of killing, it was not my time to go yet. I was destined to come back and start living on purpose. My purpose was to come back to start making sense of life and deliver the message that will determine how our story will end. It is a story of whether or not we are going to kill ourselves and our planet or if we will awaken to our super consciousness in time.

The second type of suicide is a quick suicide. The fight within you is so intense you can no longer take it. There is such a painful separation within you. You do not know what to do. You do not know what it even is. You just do not feel well in your own head and body. You cannot calm the pressure down. It is there every single day. It is with you everywhere you go. You cannot leave it behind or remove it. You do not know how to deal with it. You do not even know how to admit it. You do not know how to express it to others or to yourself. You are ashamed of the way you feel. You see that everyone else is doing great and you are the only one suffering. You feel that you must get out. So you hang yourself, take pills or shoot yourself.

In truth, you did not want to kill your real self but the false self. You wanted to shoot the false self that you have been programmed into. It was the parasite eating at you alive.

United We Stand

> "If you think we can't change the world, it just
> means you're not one of those that will."
>
> *-Jacque Fresco*

We never realize how natural love is to us until we are tested. It is usually in the most tragic and horrific situations that are brought onto us to make us understand who we truly are and what this experience we call life is about. It is to teach us that it is not the things but the relationships we have with others that matter the most. It is to teach us that our family is not only the people we share our last name with but everyone around us. It is to teach us that we are one.

Roger was a good friend of our family. Roger married his sweetheart Samantha. They were perfect for each other. They were in their late forties when they got together and were empty nesters. They appreciated a good glass of wine, relaxing and enjoying easy life. They purchased an older home in Ventura wine county of Southern California and took a pride in fixing it. It was a lovely home. Roger was a high-tech executive with a good job. He enjoyed working with wood as his hobby. He was very skilled with his hands. He built many beautiful things around the house. He completely restored the kitchen cabinets and did crown molding throughout the entire house. They also restored their beautiful pool, planted a vegetable garden, and made the garden look lovely.

Throughout the fifteen years they lived there, they completely transformed the place and it was a true labor of love for both of them. It was their baby. It was beautiful. The home was their joy, their sanctuary. It was filled with so much love. The area they lived in always had a danger of brush fires as many others along the south west coast of Pacific. It was an annual event. While living pretty close it was still always the other people this could happen to. Things one would only watch on TV as part of the news. People always hope such things will not happen to them.

Roger felt the same way. He was subconsciously aware of the danger and consciously ensuring that they will be well protected if that shall ever occur. *"I got a strong pump and it will take water all around the house from the pool. Even if all the houses around burn, my house will be safe,"* Roger used to proudly explain. He had it all figured out. He had a great plan to protect his most priced possession and their love nest. Roger did not spare expenses to ensure he was well prepared. There was no doubt in his mind that anything could go wrong.

Then the day came. It was early December when the area was experiencing Santa Ana winds. The temperatures got hot and the winds picked up. We have seen it year after year. It was only a matter of time for the fires to start from everything being so dry. It was an early hour on Tuesday morning when the police rushed into the neighborhood to wake everyone up and make them evacuate their houses. *"Everyone leaves immediately. Now!"* were the authorities ordering all the residents out of their homes. It was a mandatory emergency evacuation. *"Leave everything behind. Help the children, elderly and pets to get out. Now!"* was the chilling order of evacuation. That included also Roger and Sam's house.

The smoke was moving in and you could feel the heat from the fires. It was moving rapidly fast and there was no time for anything else nor any other thought. They had to get out. Roger had no time to get his pump going nor anything else to protect his house. Without any warning he had to abort his original plan he meticulously engineered and envisioned to protect his home.

None of that was important nor mattered. It was all about his own safety and Sam's. Fires were moving into the surrounding areas and the heat felt like being thrown into a hell. The flames were over twenty feet high and so powerful. It was overwhelming. The entire neighborhood was filled with dark smoke and unbearable heat. It was hard to breathe. People were rushing out of their beautiful homes and running down the streets. The authorities were directing the crowd towards a nearby shopping mall's parking lot. All of the neighbors gathered there.

Everyone was in disbelief. They could not grasp the reality that this is actually happening to them. That it is not just the news everyone used to watch in the safety of their living room thinking that these kind of things only happen to the other people. The moment was here. It was happening to our friends and the hundreds of their neighbors. They have never even got to know each other the years living there. Now, they were all standing there together. They were all strangers and yet so close. They were joined together through their tragedy. There was no one superior. There was no one inferior. They were all the same. They reached out and joined their hands as they were watching the tragedy unfold right in front of them.

It was the Democrat holding the Republican, the Buddhist holding the Muslim, the Christian holding the atheist and the Chinese lady holding the black man. They were all there just quietly standing, holding hands and watching the fires to claim all the beautiful houses, gardens, cars, trees and anything else that came into its powerful path of destruction. They have never met before yet they felt their bond, their strong connection. They were strangers, yet they felt like a family now. They were all standing there in the dark, wearing pajamas. Some did not even have shoes on. They were there all together, no longer separated by their status, possessions, background, nor beliefs. They joined through their hearts. They could feel such a strong connection. In that moment there was no judgment, no competition, and no hate that could possibly separate them. There was only love. Unconditional love for each other and for life in general. For most people it was an eye opening, surreal moment, and feeling of enlightenment. Somehow, in the midst of all the tragedy and suffering there was an unusual peace and unity.

Everything happens for a reason. Even tragedies like these are sent to us to make us learn about ourselves. To make us review our relationship with others. It makes us think about our actions. It makes us appraise our relationship with the environment and our planet. It only depends on how many lessons we have to receive in order to learn the lesson. That is the real question for us to think about. Tragedies and suffering will continue to happen until we are able to see through all of our mistakes and selfish behavior.

The only thing that separates us from each other is fear, belief, and ego. Your fear might be conscious or subconscious. You might be fully aware or not. You are willing to admit it or simply live in a denial because it would expose your deeply rooted ego structure. You can deny it but you cannot lie to yourself and your psyche.

The sooner you start understanding and learning about yourself the sooner you will be able to set yourself free and realize the true potential within you.

Chapter 9
SPIRITUALITY

"The great spiritual geniuses, whether it was Moses, Buddha, Plato, Socrates, Jesus or Emerson; have taught man to look within himself to find God."

-*Ernest Holmes*

Finding God

Practicing religion in my homeland of communist Czechoslovakia was not permitted. My family was Catholic but I did not grow up with religion. My family mentioned the church from time to time. They all used to go to church and were strong believers in God prior to communism. My sister and I rarely went to church. Even when I immigrated to America, organized man-made religion never made sense to me. (Please know that with the word 'religion', I am referring to the merger of the state and church to maintain power and control.)

Religious people were talking sweet words but did not follow through with their actions. I heard many emphasize their specific beliefs as it were some kind of a higher class that would help them reach higher status of salvation. Many understood it as a free pass to go about their dishonest, selfish way when no one was looking. They would come to church on Sundays, nicely dressed with their shoes nicely shined. They would pray, relieve their sins and ask for forgiveness. It was always the same week after week. I could never understand this kind of practice and for that reason, it did not make much sense to me to join. It did not feel genuine. It looked only like a nice façade. I had to be true to myself. For that reason, instead of religion I looked towards nature for my answers.

The only times I remember going to church was on Christmas Eve. We would dress up and my father would put a nice suit on. We attended Christmas mass service. Many beautiful songs were performed and it was magical. It was such a special time to me. I so much wanted to be a part of this spiritual experience. I have visited many beautiful churches not only around the Czech Republic and throughout Europe but also in Asia and Central America through my world travels. Czech Republic alone has many beautiful and impressive cathedrals. Anytime I would enter a church, however, I would always have a strange feeling.

I could not explain it but it was not a pleasant feeling. It was not necessarily a horrible feeling either. It was something in between. Whatever it was, it made me extremely emotional. It was a very bizarre emotion. It was connected with fear and suffering. I could not fully explain it. I wanted to make sense of it but did not have anyone to discuss it with. I was afraid of judgment and condemnation. I am not sure if I would even be able to explain what I felt. It was something that had remained deep inside of me for most of my life. It was almost like the powers within the walls of the church were taking over my inner powers. I did not know what to think about it.

Every time I would enter a church, I had overwhelming feelings of respect while at the same time, my throat would close up. I would feel the immense power. It made me feel very weak. I would usually cry. I would have to rush out because of the intense feelings. I could not handle it. I knew that there was some Higher Power and a Creator of everything but the organized ideology being sold never completely suited me for some reason.

There would always be a beautiful speech but it all portrayed a picture of perfection. It followed a specific ideology. It was a specific way of being and if you were not all of that then you would go to hell. I knew that I was not perfect. But I knew that I was a good person deep down. I knew that I had a big loving heart. I knew that I was filled with love and compassion. I also knew that I make mistakes sometimes. Not that I wanted to but it was inevitable when my ego-driven mind got in the way.

I knew that while I had always tried to be nice I had also done some not-so-nice things. I was not always honest. I was not always the kindest. I might have even taken something that did not belong to me. I might have taken advantage possibly. I have always tried my best but I have not always succeeded. Maybe I had a bad day and was tired. Maybe I did not have a good night's rest and was cranky. I might not have been the nicest person to someone who did not deserve it. Did that make me less of a good person on a great scale of things? I never thought so.

It all came together after my near death experience. It was a slow buildup of all the events in my life that led me to the connection I was missing so much in life. I was spiritually starved. It was a connection with my higher consciousness and through that a connection to the Great Divine, God – the divine energy and everything there is. The mystical, majestic, and the powerful.

For the longest time I have been trying to put a name to it or find some kind of explanation for others to relate and understand. I wanted to tell them so that they could also find it for themselves. This was the point in my life that I realized how limited our words and symbols truly are. There is so much more than mere words can ever illustrate. It is sort of like trying to explain the feeling of love to someone who has never experienced it. Or to explain the crystal blue sky to a blind person who has never seen it. Or to explain the aroma of a rose to a person who cannot smell it.

> "The only source of knowledge is experience."
> -*Albert Einstein*

It is simply impossible to truly know God just from stories or teachings that you hear. It will make you a wonderful professor but never the master. You will always have to worship and bow to someone else's experience and discovery. You might know a lot of details on the subject but it will remain just a theory. You have to experience it. You have to become it to truly know. There is no other true knowing than one's own experience.

It is the same as if you based your understanding of the taste of banana on what a monkey, a snake and a fish told you. Each of them would tell you something different. The monkey would tell you what a delicious banana it was. The snake might tell you how tasteless it was while the fish would not even consider looking at it. They would narrate to you their different experiences. You will be able to derive your own conclusions and write a great thesis on the subject but you will still not know what a banana truly tastes like.

Anything one has not experienced personally is only based on assumptions and beliefs of others. And as you can see, those experiences can be of a rather wide range. It depends on who tells the story. The other issue would arise when you take those banana stories farther down the line, to the fourth, fifth or even the eighth generation of the monkey, snake and fish. Now the story would resemble a completely different tale than its own original version. Words or even entire books would go missing as was found when the Dead Sea Scrolls were discovered outside of Jerusalem in late 1940s. Over forty books dating back some two thousand years were found that had never made it into the current version of the Bible.

Sometimes, words were also misspelled or even entirely dropped in the copying process; this is what has happened in the past. This was the time of no printers and no copy machines. Everything was copied by human hand. Since we are humans ourselves, we know what kind of a day at work we can have after spending the entire night arguing with our spouse or dealing with a bad cold knowing we would have to pull it through the next day.

Simply put, mistakes will happen that can have significant consequences. Missing a single word *"not"* can go from *"One shall not commit adultery"* to ordering exactly the opposite as it happened in one of the Bible translations. That was only one word! Now imagine what happens when forty books go missing! This is how it goes with storytelling versus a personal experience.

The place our masters have been trying to lead us to is a state of enlightenment and awakening. It is the state of the highest consciousness through unconditional love. When you love you maintain your divine realization while living an *ordinary* life. It is the highest realization of the Self that transforms your *ordinary* life into an extraordinary one. Your mind becomes still and your body is filled with unconditional love and peace. Suddenly, everything feels amazing and beautiful. Regular chores become a privilege. Every day becomes a blessing. Your entire existence turns into a miracle.

Once you become enlightened, you cannot fall back into the same old delusion. You reach a personal relationship with the Great Divine whereas a man-made belief system is only a mind and crowd control. Many might think of it as some kind of a sect. This confusion is only due to fear of the unknown. It is the fear of being manipulated. Truthful information might threaten the established subconscious programming. To fully understand this, one must open their mind and move above the known to realize that spirituality is nothing mysterious nor is it connected to any sect. It is simply about connecting to the higher Self.

Throughout my travels and discussions with regular people from different religious backgrounds, I would always find the same ideology and concept recurring deep down. It was an unconditional love that bound all beliefs together. It was only the different stories, which they taught, and the state of fear that took humanity away from the founding knowledge. These were stories that followed a specific ideology and told to obey certain rules. If you did not follow these rules there would be punishment.

On the other hand, spirituality teaches to ascend the mind and follow the heart. It shows you to do what is right, which is something that no one needs to teach you. You do know deep inside the difference between good and bad by your natural instinct. Spirituality sets you free to be your real self without bowing to anyone nor anything that does not resonate as correct with you. Spirituality trusts your inner divinity. It respects the choices that you make because it knows you will always honor and do good sooner or later. Man-made construct of beliefs, conversely, uses the fear of punishment. It creates a force because they know that through fear, you will obey and conform to the specific rules that they have set.

Spirituality does not focus on fear; instead, it makes you aware of the consequences through love. It empowers all the good within you. It teaches you how to live without fear. It guides you to make correct choices. It accepts the mistakes you might make along the journey because it is what makes you learn and improve. It is what makes you a human. Spirituality inspires you to act on unconditional love and not on fear.

Spirituality encourages you to learn yourself, discover yourself and accept yourself as the unique, divine being you are. It motivates you to connect to your higher Self. It lets you see the truth as whole - the truth which is the same for each of us. It shows you that we are One. It allows for your own individuality to shine and through that, it helps you believe in your own truth, through your own perception, guided by your powerful heart.

There are over four thousand religions in the world. They all preach their own belief. They preach to their audience that their belief is the right belief. Spirituality does not use separation but unity as it sees the deep truth in all of them despite our uniqueness and differences. Spirituality does not emphasize the differences but the underlying divine message that all religions share. It does not focus on the details of the tale that each of them tell. It only inspires to connect through our hearts to higher consciousness.

Living in Hell

> "If you suffer, it is because of you. If you feel blissful, it is because of you. Nobody else is responsible, only you and you alone. You are your own hell and heaven too."
>
> *-Osho*

I was traveling on a business trip with John. I was looking forward to it. Business trips were exciting. I would not only get to meet customers, get out of the office but also get to know my colleagues better. There was something about business trips that made me know people on a completely different level. It is when you travel and spend an extended period of time together outside of the controlled office settings that you can learn more about people.

John was in his early fifties with strong religious beliefs. He was divorced with two children. We had busy days working and then we had interesting deep discussions in the evenings. We had a great time. Our discussions were never dull and were always filled with excitement and energy. As time progressed, we realized that there were certain points we did not agree on. We made a silent agreement that we would simply agree to disagree. We were exploring each other's views and perceptions. It was interesting to see the maturity in our conversations. Most people would either end the conversation, change the subject or get angry when it came to something that questioned their belief system. There was a nice flow and delightful depth between John and I.

"I have a close relationship with God," John would tell me on several occasions. I had heard that comment before. It was always a bit surprising to me why there had to be such an emphasis on the fact. It is not like we go around and tell people that we have a close relationship with our spouse or anyone we are truly connected with. We just have it and we enjoy it. There is no need to highlight it unless there is a specific necessity. That specific need might be our urge to get validation or salvation. *"That's great, John,"* I answered as I became curious about his God. *"Tell me more about your God, please,"* I was excited to learn about his special relationship.

"He is perfect. He knows the best and he guides me," John continued. *"What defines being perfect and knowing the best, John?"* I asked. *"He is heavenly and he does not sin,"* he replied. *"He came down to save us and look over humanity because we, humans sin,"* he provided a detailed

explanation. *"What kind of sins are you referring to?"* I had to ask the question. *"Well, you know we do bad things in our life,"* John was opening up. I could feel a substantial sorrow hiding deep inside of him. *"I know. We do not always make the best choices but these mistakes are lessons. They were put in our journey for us to learn. These lessons came for us to grow. It is the natural path of progress. Nothing we have done is a life sentence,"* I replied.

I could feel that John was dealing with a great suffering. I could feel that it was preventing him from forgiving himself in order to reach the inner peace that he was yearning for so much. I could see such a beautiful and loving person in him. I could see the sin that he was carrying. That sin created a prison for him in his own mind. I could feel how much love he wanted to give to the world but he could not. He was not free. There was a wall built between his inner and outer world. This wall was blocking him from being all he ever wanted to be. John could feel it but did not know how to climb over this wall. He did not know how to forgive himself in order to let his divine light shine through. It created an inner pressure and anxiety in him for the sake of his perfect God who never sins. I could feel the unresolved pain within him.

I needed to help John out of his prison. *"You know, John, labeling and judging is one of the most damaging things we can do. What one considers normal could be offensive and a sin to another. Look at me right now. I am wearing a tight pair of jeans and a laced top with a pretty deep cut. I guarantee you that according to certain conservative cultures, I would be committing a sin. I would be evil. It would be their subjective perception and a result of their cultural conditioning."* I continued the discussion.

"Even though I wouldn't be thrilled about their perception I cannot be upset with them either. The reason being is that I come from love. With that, I do understand where their reasoning is coming from. At the same time,

though, I will not be ashamed of myself due to their cultural perception. I would not feel guilt or any shame because I am fully aware of the responsibility I carry over myself. That responsibility extends only to me and my being only. I own my body. How much or how little I show is my business only. My body is a divine gift to my spirit. What others think of it is their business. My responsibility stops right there. I can never control other people's thoughts or perceptions," I told to him. I was trying to explain to John that no one could oversee or judge me unless I let them to do so.

We all came from love and are divine. There is only an inner fight between the ego and the higher Self. The higher Self knows itself whereas the ego is insecure because it is based on beliefs. The ego continuously feels threatened. It constantly looks for self-justification and approval of others. It is based on uncertainty, doubt and fear. Because of that, it needs to compete, control, and manipulate. It needs to continuously and relentlessly prove itself. It needs others for self-gratification and validation. It is nothing without others. It takes away a person's inner peace and replaces it with a battle. This inner battle will continue until a person realizes what is truly going on in his inner world. Peace can never exist in this kind of environment.

"*I can see your point,*" said John, "*But what if a married man cheats on his wife with a prostitute because he is not getting any attention at home?*" he burst out just like that. He was surprised himself at what he had just said. I knew without a doubt that he was referring to himself. He had cheated on his wife with a prostitute. He needed sex that he did not get from his marital contract. His wife found out and divorced him. He not only lost his family but his entire life. He became a rejected being. He committed a sin in his God's eyes. He became a bad man forever. Because of his religious beliefs he might spend the rest of his life in regret and self-disgrace. He voluntarily put himself in a prison with a life sentence with no chance of parole.

SPIRITUALITY

How tragic. I could feel John's pain. He willingly turned his life into a suffering over a mistake. He was marked for the rest of his life. His life had turned into a living hell with hopes for heaven in another life. I just wanted to hug John and never let go. I could see his inner child who was starved of love. I wanted to tell him that things are not as he was made to believe. I wanted him to know what a beautiful person he is. I wanted him to know that this was just a mistake, not a condemnation for life.

All this pain was sitting inside of him like a large boulder that was breached in the flow of his life energy. It was so large and unbearable. It filled his entire existence with self-imposed shame, betrayal and guilt because of an illusion.

He felt that his life was over and the opportunity to become a good man long gone. It only happened because he was comparing himself to his God who was so perfect. His God's worship was his blessing and curse at the same time. John was so dependent on someone else's tale that got misinterpreted. Without being aware of it, this wrong belief was disabling him. It was making him paralyzed. It was making him sick. John could never be as good as his God. He could never have the same powers while Jesus specifically wanted him to know that he would be able to do even greater things than him.

It was a tragic discovery for me to see what a belief can do to a person. It locks them up, incarcerating themselves. They are forever a victim of their own mistakes. John was so sure that humanity was full of sins and for that they can never be as good as his God. He was made believe that only God can take him to heaven after he dies. He did not know that we were born into heaven.

"*Where is heaven, John?*" I asked, full of curiosity. He turned his eyes up to the sky. "*It is where God came from and where we will eventually go if we can serve him,*" he answered, full of hope for the next point in his journey. I could feel the excitement and anticipation from him for the future that would come after his life here.

It was the promise of heaven. That promise made him completely disregard the present moment as though it was not even here. John was condemned to only serve his master now in hopes that he could go to heaven later. John was just surviving the days while here in this beautiful life experience. His days were spent in suffering and dreaming for the promise of a better future which would never come.

John was powerless over his destiny. It was all up to his master, his judgment and guidance. I felt sad for him because he had no idea how powerful and heavenly he actually could be if only he let go of the mind ruling. It was years and generations of programming stamped into his blood. It was overpowering his entire existence.

We are the Universe and the Universe is us. Our body is a tiny speck of dust filled with empty space. That empty space is not empty at all. It is filled with so much. It is filled with higher intelligence and our connection to the Creation. It is the Holy Spirit, the Great Divine, Quantum Hologram, God or whatever other name you wish to use to describe it. It is expressing itself through our consciousness. It is the center of the Universe that controls and holds everything together. It is the divine energy of life. It is an unconditional love. It is a life source we have cut ourselves from. That is why there is so much suffering, so much pain. That is why there is so much disease in the humankind, unlike any other species on this planet. In order to heal ourselves and our planet we have to reconnect. We must reconnect back to love.

It is that connection and the constant exchange of information that goes back and forth. It is what gives us life. The Universe has been so patient and so loving to us. It carries all its functions and creations through unconditional love. That's what the Universe is made of. The

Universe only pretends to be made out of matter. It is the limited view of the naked eye and illusions of the mind that make us believe otherwise. Secretly, the Universe is made of love. This sacred energy is pulling us. It wants us to quiet down the mind and open our hearts. It is where we tune in to the God within us.

> "Enlightenment is when a wave realizes it is the ocean."
> -*Thich Nhat Hanh*

United In Love

> "To love is to recognize yourself in another."
> -*Eckhart Tolle*

On December 2, 2016, close to midnight a fire broke out in a warehouse in Oakland, California. The flames took over the structure. It was impossible for the firefighters to get to the victims in time. Thirty-six people were killed in the fire. It was the deadliest fire in the history of Oakland at that time. It was a horrible, unimaginable event. Horrible chills went through my entire body when I read the news. I disconnected mentally from what I was doing and connected with the victims inside.

I could feel the intense heat and the fear from the unavoidable fire. Words cannot describe what I felt for the people I had never met. It was not just news to me; it was as if my family members were burning there. A few family members of the fire victims received distressed phone calls from their loved ones. They were calls to say their final goodbye. The victims trapped inside were complete strangers. They were of different descent, religion, sex, and race. No one was thinking about their differences at their final moments, though. They ascended those thoughts and programming. They ascended their mind.

They all gathered. They hugged each other to comfort each other as the flames and the unimaginable death through suffering approached them. They all put aside their social conditioning. They put aside their race. They put aside their gender. They put aside their status and their religion. They came together through love and became a family. They became ONE in the final hours of their life. They were no longer thinking through their minds but feeling through their most powerful hearts.

They no longer had their ego, religion, or fear separating them. There was an absolute unity. Despite the horrible tragedy and their unimaginable end, they were filled with unconditional love. They found support with one another in the final hour. They were all killed but they had each other. They found unconditional love that created a bridge between them and everything else.

It is a catastrophic story. It is not the only story that has ever happened. It happens quite often that in the most difficult times, we put aside our differences and become connected again. The only question remains, why do we have to wait for such dramatic, tragic times to do so? I think we have plenty of tragedies, wars and conflicts to learn from. I think it is time that we open our hearts and instead of fearing our lives away, we start loving. It is much better that way. It is so much healthier that way. You take my word for it.

I used to fear everything in my life. Almost anything and everything could go wrong. So many possibilities and possibilities within those possibilities. The list was endless. I had fear and stress controlling my life. There was danger on every corner and I was driving myself insane worrying about it. Through the fear and stress, I built an intense resistance towards life. I put myself into a dis-ease state without even realizing it. Everything seemed such a struggle. Life was struggle and a never-ending worry.

Then I started to realize that most of the things I was stressing over and worrying about would never happen. When I let go of all the fear, I made a connection to the higher Self. I found my way to the Great Divine and a new world opened up to me. Suddenly I was living in a world filled with abundance, love and peace. It was still the same world; what had changed was my perception. I zoomed in on the details and the everyday miracles that we overlook because we take them for granted.

Deeper Truth

"Love is the most durable power in the world."
-Martin Luther King, Jr.

One of my biggest discoveries was to learn that there is no such thing as good or evil. Things just are. It is not until we label and judge them that they become evil or good. A friend of mine pointed out Adolf Hitler as an example of evil. What happened during the Nazi era was catastrophic, without a doubt. My hometown was heavily occupied by the Nazis. My direct family was affected. Several of our family members were killed. Our family house was confiscated. Hitler and his actions personally affected me. But perhaps, the truth about evil goes a bit deeper and requires closer examination.

I am pretty much sure that baby Adolf's aspiration was not to become a genocide legend. I do not think that any baby for the fact would want to be anything of that sort. Love comes naturally to us. It is hate that is taught. With that, one has to wonder, what happened to that innocent baby. What possibly led to the following tragic events? This is crucial to examine before we engage in any type of judgment. Most don't know that Adolf Hitler came from a physically and mentally abusive family. It was Adolf's father that made his childhood a living hell.

Adolf loved to paint. All he wanted was to become an artist. Unfortunately, he didn't find the needed resources or support since his parents died early on. Desperate to survive in difficult times of great depression in Germany, he joined the army. He found his purpose in war. He was awarded many medals for his bravery serving his country. He almost died in a gas attack that left him blind for a week. Through his military conditioning he was built into a strong nationalist. He believed in his country more than anything else. His country became his passion. It became his purpose. This was all shaken when Germany lost the war in 1918. Hitler was made to believe by others that it was the communist party and the Jews that presented a great threat to his beloved country.

He took it as his devotion to his country to make Germany great again. You might recall an American presidential candidate using the same slogan: *"To make America great again."* But perhaps if this "bad" seed of Hitler was planted in a fertile soil flooded with love and compassion, he might have become the next Picasso or Monet. We would have never experienced the Holocaust and all the tragic events under his horrific ruling. How tragic. How unfortunate. One has to wonder. Why do things really happen as they do? Is there possibly a deeper meaning for us to see? Where was God and His protection when millions were being tortured and murdered? Where is the holy justice? What does it all mean?

It is like this because the events are there to teach us. They are there to hit us in the head and say *"wake up!"* It is there to show us what family abuse and trauma can possibly do to an individual. What nationalism can do when millions blindly follow a single leader. How many millions can be murdered and put through inhumane suffering because of a belief. Was it really just the actual person or was it the system and conditioning? Was it just a person or rather the nationalistic belief that one country or nation is superior over another?

It was all only possible because the love of power took over the power of love. It was only possible because millions of humans were lost in a blind pursuit of ideology. It was the same erroneous thinking we have practiced now for so many generations. When are we going to finally learn?

It is fascinating how our brain and belief system works. It is even more fascinating how it can be hijacked when enlightenment has not been achieved. Everything is connected to everything else. We live in a connected world. It is referred to as the Divine Matrix or Quantum Hologram. In this Quantum Hologram, there is a footprint for life itself with all its possibilities referred to as parallel universes.

It contains all the intelligence that controls our Universe and all there is. This intelligence has only one thing in mind: life-affirming functions. These functions are always loving. This intelligence is all about life and reproduction. It never creates any life-denying actions.

Since it is always pro-life, there is never a conflict or friction. It is by design. Even the dark is needed for times to rest and rejuvenate. It is time for things to be reset in order to recharge and function again. It is one flowing continuum that will take you before and beyond the Bing Bang.

Our planet went through five massive extinctions. One of them wiped out as much as eighty seven percent of life. Yet the universal intelligence managed to recreate life on this planet again. How amazing! What a miracle! We are, however, headed for the sixth massive extinction at the current state of affairs. We have boarded the Titanic and are heading for an iceberg. That iceberg can be nuclear, bio-chemical or environmental. Albert Einstein described it clearly when he was asked about the third world war. He said that he cannot comment on the third world war but can make a prediction about the fourth. It was a puzzling answer.

"How can you predict fourth world war and say nothing about the third?" he was asked. He answered that there will not be any fourth world war because the third one would completely destroy the entire existence on earth. We are living in times unlike any other. We are standing on an edge. We are the generation that will make a difference. A difference of being remembered as the murderers of Earth or the angels of Heaven. The good news is that planet Earth will be perfectly fine without us. Based on the current state of our collective affairs, one would even suggest it will be much better without us.

This is the heaven on Earth. It is everywhere around us and within us if only we decide to claim it. We can change this world like turning a switch tomorrow. All we have to do is unite and decide that enough is enough! We all carry this power and higher intelligence within us. We are the conscious manifestation of the Universe itself. It is time to ascend the material world driven by fear, greed, jealousy and competition and join a world driven by unconditional love.

Love is our natural state of being. Hate has to be learnt. That's the deepest truth. The only question remains, how much have we learnt from World War II, Hiroshima and all the other wars? Have we concluded yet that wars and killing can never lead to anything positive? How many more millions of our children will we need to sacrifice before we get it? The last century was the darkest time for humanity. Close to one hundred and eighty seven million humans were killed by their own fellow humans. And yet, we still engage in killings and wars that we fight over difference in beliefs, race, borders and political views. This only creates a deeper level of separation between us. This is the true purpose of politics and world religion.

War is only good for political ratings and big business. There are no heroes nor is there any glory in war. Heroes are those who prevent war through love and compassion. When are we going to understand that war can never bring peace? It is the same logic as screaming for silence or having sex for virginity. Only peace can produce peace. It is the peace that starts from within that is a product of love not only for ourselves but for others as well.

Chapter 10

TIME IS JUST AN ILLUSION

"Yesterday is a history. Tomorrow is a mystery but today is a gift. That's why it is called the present."

-Unknown

Time Mystery

If I asked you what is time, what would you say? We do not really think about time. Yet, we live in it. We live with time every moment, every day of our lives. It is everywhere around us – every day, every moment of our existence. According to the dictionary, time is a component quantity of various measurements used to sequence events. It is to compare the duration of events or the intervals between them. It is used to quantify rates of change of quantities in material reality or in the conscious experience. Physics is the only science that explicitly studies time. Many physicists studying this phenomena agree that time is one of the most difficult properties of our Universe to understand.

I trust you have had an experience where the exact five minutes in one situation were not the same as the five minutes in another situation. Five minutes of sitting in a dental chair having a root canal done feels like eternity. Then take the exact quantity of time, the same five minutes, which you used to do something enjoyable, like making love or playing with your kids on the beach. It was exactly the same quantity of time but the experience you had varied greatly. Five minutes felt like an eternity in one situation, while in the other, it felt like a split of second.

Time is one of the biggest mysteries of your existence. It makes sense to understand it since you cannot escape it. It is when you slow down and start to notice that you make more of time. When you slow down you notice the world around you. You are able to zoom in. It is when you quiet down the mind and go deeply into the thought of time that you realize that time does not really exist. Think about it. No one owns it. No one has it. You can only create it. It is a true mastery to train the brain to perceive time as such and understand the power of now.

Past is what happened and it is now long gone. Past is just a sequence of images running from your memory. Some memories are good and some are bad. Some things you remember and some you do not. Most the times, you remember the bad times. It is because those bad memories inflicted pain of some kind. They were like sharp pieces of glass that created painful scars that got stored in your subconscious mind. Your mind was designed like this with a purpose to protect you, make you learn and grow from that painful experience. That is all what it was supposed to do.

Yet, so many become trapped in the past and attach themselves to their pain-body. It becomes their new identity. It becomes attached to your ego and it becomes you. It is a dark shadow cast of your ego. Like any other identity, the pain-body needs to survive. It can be nourished only by an experience that resonates with the same vibrational energy. It is anything that keeps you in pain through emotions such as anger, violence, pity, doubt and any kind of drama. Pain is nourished only by pain. It cannot be nourished by love or joy. In fact, love and joy cannot be swallowed by the pain-body.

When you are absorbed by the pain-body, you want more pain. You unconsciously seek pain because it evokes familiar feelings and you seek the familiar, the known. The familiar feelings make you feel alive. You become a victim or a culprit of pain. You want it either through inflicting pain on others or suffering through pain yourself or both. Because this is happening unconsciously, you are naturally not aware of this phenomenon. With that, when you read this, you will argue that you do not want pain. The pain-body is scared of the truth that can be only realized through a light of consciousness.

It is important to remember that the past is done business. Now, you have a choice. You can spend a lifetime thinking over the past. You can dwell over the issues, situations, and people that hurt you. When you do this, all you are really doing is opening your wounds and bringing the same pain up to the surface again. You would never do that with an actual, physical wound so why do that with a mental wound? It is literally like digging into a scar you got when you crashed your bike at the age of ten years. The wound is nicely healed now with new skin formed over it. You can hardly see the scar with your eyes. But you want to feel it again. You want to experience the same pain over and over again so you take a knife and start cutting it open.

It makes absolutely no sense. You are literally reliving those moments over and over again. You can spend twenty years or the rest of your life revisiting your past hurts and all those that wronged you. You can analyze, scrutinize, and try to make sense of things. As you keep doing that, you will find out that the deeper you go, the more there is for you to find and agonize over. All this process of tearing up old wounds gives you is the strength to feel more victimized and continue to have one big pity party after another.

You have an option. Instead of doing this, you can rise higher. Realize that what happened is no longer here. Make peace with it. Learn from it. Take action. Imagine yourself stepping away from your past. Imagine giving up what you no longer want, what is no longer serving you. You are not your past. You are your future. Envision yourself living in joy and love. Pain is the story of the past and it has nothing more to offer you. You've got it now. You learned your lesson. Now is the time to forgive. It is the time to imagine a different life ahead of you. It is the time of bliss and forever honeymoon.

Forgive not only those who hurt you but also forgive yourself. You are the same child like everyone else. We are all just little kids learning. We are all just trying to figure out this thing called life. That is why we make mistakes so we can learn and grow. This is what makes us all such beautiful, divine beings. It is what makes us human rather than robots of precision. No one is perfect and forgiveness is the greatest gift you can give.

It is true that some people will not deserve your forgiveness and it is perfectly fine. Learn how to give it anyway. Learn how to overcome the initial resistance. When you do, you will create a beautiful space for peace and love that will fill your body. Dark energy of fear will no longer be blocking you. It will not only feel much better but you will heal yourself through this process as well. As you keep practicing this, you will realize that it also gives you power over your emotions.

There is a great power and strength when you become in charge of your thoughts and the way you feel. It is when you do not let others to affect your inner peace. Forgiveness is a gift to yourself because you deserve happiness.

Focus and live in the now because it is the only place where life exists. Time is like a river. It just flows. You can never touch the same water twice. The only thing you can do is to enjoy the now, live in it and make the most of it. Realize its power because that is where the magic happens. Life is built of now until there is another now and then another and so on. You have never experienced anything in past. It was only the now of that specific moment. You will never have the same moment more than once. Enjoy it and nourish it because it will never be here again.

I was lucky to learn this pretty early on without even being aware of it. Every enjoyable moment I had, I would soak it in. I just embraced each moment and each second. As I practiced this, I made these moments feel like eternity. I would notice all the smells, the colors, the people, the animals, the setting – every single thing. I learned how to zoom in to things and make the moment last longer than it truly was. It was almost as if I stopped the clock for myself.

On the other hand, when I looked around I saw others rushing around in panic like they had some other place to be than this life. They were in such a big panic as if it were mandatory to achieve something beyond themselves. They were rushing through their precious moments as if they were going to get out of this life alive. It was almost comical because I used to be the same. I was killing myself and rushing through my life like I had somewhere else to be. It was almost surreal how I was cheating myself out of the best things in life.

This rush and anxiousness is the underlying fear of the unknown and anticipation for a future that never arrives. It is an illusion and a direct projection from the pain-filled past that keeps us in panic. It makes us feel like we are in a situation of constant threat and fear. Life turns into a struggle and we feel that we can never get ahead. We see everyone but ourselves achieving and finding the forever happiness. We end up living in chronic fear.

This is the fear of the unknown, the fear of what might come. It revolves around the thought that what may come might not be good. There are all the ominous possibilities running through our minds: an earthquake can strike, money can run out, job might be lost, our spouse can leave us or someone might get sick. It is a forever running scenarios of things that might go wrong though ninety nine percent of the time, none of that does ever happen.

Once again, it is the subconscious mind playing tricks on us. We have to stop this little voice in our heads because everything will be okay in the end. It always is; and if it is not, I guess it is not the end. Just think about it for a moment. Stop the madness. Stop constantly building for the future at the cost of the current moment. Do not miss all the possible opportunities that the present moment offers to you.

Memory Never Lived

> "The key to growth is the introduction of higher dimensions of consciousness into our awareness."
>
> *-Lao Tzu*

I had the best realization of time and its relativity during a summer vacation in Hawaii. My boys were just little. We left our hotel to explore the Big Island. I always loved to show my children new things and explore with them. We were visiting one of the most beautiful waterfall areas. We purchased a brand new video camera to capture the exciting vacation so that we could replay it at a later time. I was in charge of the filming.

With the camera in my hands, I filmed my family and the surroundings. I was making a movie to capture the amazing times. We wanted to preserve these exciting memories forever. We wanted to bottle the experience so we could just go back to it and get another piece from the jar. We finished our exploration and came back to the car. My family was full of excitement, talking about how amazing the views and the waterfalls were. It was in that moment that it hit me: I had no such feelings.

I did not feel the same high nor was I super excited like the rest of my family. With my eyes attached to the camera and my mind focused on the recording job I had completely missed on the actual experience. I never got to live it. I was just a bystander. I was just there taking pictures and recording a video but I did not truly live through the experience. I completely missed out on the precious moment of excitement with my boys. I am sure I made a great video that captured of it all but for me, personally, I had missed on a moment that I could never get back. I saw everything only through one lens of the camera. It was almost like I was not even there.

I have never forgotten this experience and the feeling it left inside of me. I was filled with sadness and regret for the lost moment. I felt robbed. This was a moment that I will never be able to get again. While I was sad, I was also grateful. I was thankful for the lesson. It was profound and it made me appreciate life so much more. From that point on, I did not care about taking videos or taking pictures that much. What became more important to me was living in each moment fully and being at the highest level of consciousness.

I wanted to experience every second of my life to its fullest extent, no matter where I was. Who knows, it might be my last day today and I want to make sure that it is the best day!

Time is elusive. If we do not capture every moment of the present, one day we might be only left with regrets. The only thing you can do is be in the now. See everything around you, experience every minute and indulge in each moment. Do this through deep, meditative exploration. Learn how to see because there is so much to see. 'Now' is eternal; it stops the clock if you learn how to just *be*. It is a gift and that is why it is called the present.

Procrastination

> "Procrastination is the thief of time."
>
> -*Edward Young*

Procrastination is the best self-pleasing and self-sabotage agenda the mind could have ever invented. *"I don't have time to detox because I have a business trip that I have to take,"* or *"I have to get my kid to college,"* or *"I have to take care of my sick mother first,"* and the list just goes on and on. What it means you don't have time to take care and be in charge of your health. I would hear this in my practice so often. Do you ever notice that this list is never ending? We are super creative when it comes to finding excuses for something we need to do but do not want to. Somehow, we are all waiting for the right time but time doesn't seem to wait for us! What a paradox!

    The explanation is very simple. It is because time does not exist. Time is the biggest illusion of all. I am talking about the illusion that somehow the right time will magically appear at your doorstep, ring the bell and say, *"Here I am!"* It is a rather ridiculous misconception but it is what we are all secretly hoping for. This type of thinking keeps you living in the past. What happens is that the images of the past are projected onto the future while the now slips right through your fingers.

Till Death Us Apart

> "Life and death are one thread, the same line viewed from different sides."
>
> -Lao Tzu

When I met Clay, it was a love at first sight. He was strong and confident. His body was muscular and he had a fearless look in his eyes. I was immediately drawn to him. I knew that he was meant to be with me and there was no question about it. I knew that Clay was bringing something special in my life. *"So, do you think that you can adopt him?"* asked Judith who was fostering Clay for a few days while he was recovering from a kennel cough. *"Absolutely, there is no doubt about it,"* I and the rest of my family replied.

It was almost a year since our previous dog had died. We knew it was time to give another deserving soul a home and a second chance. It took us quite some time to get over the loss. We had our dog for eight years, ever since he was a tiny puppy. He was a little brother to my kids and we all loved him dearly. He died suddenly from a heart attack. It was like losing a family member. It took us almost a full year to consider welcoming another dog to our family. This time, though, we were not going to buy a puppy but were going to rescue one instead. It made the whole family feel so good on the inside.

We had always wanted to rescue a dog. There was something very satisfying in a rescue. I never looked at these dogs as broken or as damaged goods. On the contrary, I viewed them as very strong souls that have experienced immense diversity. They have lived through many experiences, unlike other dogs. They had to fight very hard to keep up their spirit to survive. If they were human, we would call them strong and admirable. We would call them heroes. They would have so many amazing stories to tell. We all would admire their incredible strength, courage, and faith.

We made a trip to the local shelter. It was an exciting moment for the entire family. I was a bit scared of how I would feel seeing all the dogs that needed a home but I gathered all my courage. I told myself to be strong. Ever since I was a little child, I had a very soft spot for anyone in need, especially for animals that depend on us so much. When we got there, we walked through the cages and looked at all the dogs. They were well taken care of and in very nice condition. Then we spotted Joey.

He was a brown pit bull. *"Mom, can we please take Joey home?"* begged my youngest son. *"I think we can, baby. Let's go to fill out the application,"* I replied with confidence. When we got to the office they accepted our application but told us that there are other people who have also applied for him. *"We will review your application and will let you know in couple of days,"* said the lovely lady behind the counter.

It was a wait of two long days. I was bit surprised that they had so many people interested in adopting Joey. It was a pleasant surprise actually, and made me feel hopeful that all the dogs will get a new home. I did want to make sure, however, that my boys were ready in case we did not get Joey. *"Everything happens for a reason, boys,"* I told my sons while we were waiting for the news. *"If Joey is meant to be with us, he will. If he is meant to be with another family he will not come to be with us. You need to understand that it is not about us but about Joey and his well-being. If we do not get him and another family does instead then you have to be happy for Joey,"* I explained to my children.

I wanted to make sure that they understood what this was about. I wanted them to learn and practice unconditional love by putting their interests aside. *"We know, mom. It is all about Joey. But if we do not get him can we look for another dog please?"* they asked. *"Of course we will look for another dog!"* I responded. Ultimately, we did not get Joey. Then one day, we found a white muscular boxer online. There was a message attached that said that he was in desperate need of home.

He was rescued from a high kill shelter. We applied and before we knew it we got him. His name was Clay. Bringing him home was not easy. He was seventy pounds of restless muscle jumping all over us. The one-hour car ride home seemed to last forever. Clay was like a tiger in a cage. He just hated the ride. It was exhausting trip. We were happy to arrive home. We brought Clay to his new home. The entire family was happy and excited to have a new family member. He was beautiful and a much larger dog than the ones we had in the past. We made him a nice bed and fed him.

Clay checked the house and our garden out. He looked less stressed, as if he was ready to relax. When we got Clay he was pretty skinny for his size. It was my immediate goal to get him well quick. I could hardly go to sleep the first night from the excitement to have rescued such a beautiful dog. I just wanted to play with him the entire night. It felt so good to have a dog again and one that was getting a second chance on life. In the following days, my bond with Clay grew stronger. There was something mystical about him and his soul that drew me in. I think it was the confidence and assurance energy he projected.

Clay knew who he was and he was not easily convinced to go against what he wanted. He was stubborn but had a very kind and loving heart. He did not like other dogs, however, and that had made it very hard for people to adopt him. I learned very quickly how bad it was when he broke away from his collar and tried to attack another dog when we took him for a hike.

That was his first day with us. We quickly realized that he had a major issue with other dogs. We realized that our new dog was a bait dog in the past used for fighting. It was a sad realization but something we had to accept and deal with. We were not going to give up on him. We simply had to train him and keep tight control over him. In time, I was hopeful that we would show him a different way of being through love.

I was determined that Clay had his second chance. He was not easy. He broke about every window screen in the house, damaged a couple of sofas and wrecked both of our cars. He started to jump our six feet tall fence and even got into doggie jail a couple of times. We had police call us to rush home to get our dog because he was standing on the roof of our house and was about to jump. Times with Clay were unlike anything we had ever experienced but we were determined. We loved him unconditionally until his last breath, which unfortunately came way before his time was due.

Clay had to be only three years old and we had him only five months when he started to lose weight and his appetite. I took him to a vet and got the bad news: Clay had lymphoma. This was the same type of cancer as I've developed. We all cried. I could not believe the news. I was mad at the world. I mustered all my strength and decided that we were going to beat this. It was what I had done for myself. Clay was going to heal. I saw it as the reason why he came to me. For the following three weeks, I made him raw food with every possible cancer-fighting superfood ingredients. We did reiki, deep meditation, lymphatic massage and vibrational therapy just to mention few.

During this time, everything was about Clay. We made every expenditure to get him only the best holistic care. Clay was a great patient but he knew that he was leaving. He no longer had the strength to survive and I could feel it. I knew it. It was the hardest thing for me to accept. I was the one fighting for his life. It was a battle I could never win. It was all about me while Clay was ready to return home. He stopped eating on Friday. I was determined to keep fighting as long as he could take his water. I was hoping that his body was just going into the last stage of cancer starvation before he would bounce back just as I had done a few years ago.

I came home from work on Monday afternoon. It was day twenty of Clay's treatment. He could no longer stand up. His muscular seventy-pound body resembled a skeleton now. We had to pick him up and carry him to the garden to do his business. He was tired and slept a lot. He opened his eyes tiredly when I got home. He looked straight into my eyes. I saw that his eyes were clear and they were saying: *"Mommy, it is time for me to go. I love you very much and I am grateful I got to meet you all. Thank you for giving me such a loving home and believing in me. I will forever remember the unconditional love I was able to experience. Please do not mourn for me. Please keep your heart and this loving home open for another soul in need."*

It was hard but I had to finally accept the inevitable. It was time for Clay to go. It was his journey and it was ending. I told my family and they slept with him. Clay passed away in their arms at 2 am in the morning.

It was as if time stopped - there was just a huge void. I wanted Clay back so badly. Just one more day, one more hike, one more broken window screen. I would give anything to have our troublemaker back. Suddenly, his troubles turned into blessings in its own special way. Later, we often laughed over the great adventures that we got to experience through Clay. It was also the experience to see life and death unfolding in front of our eyes. It was such a meaningful lesson for my children to see how precious life is, what disease can do and the salvation death delivers.

I never forgot what Clay told me. Only two days later we saved another amazing soul that was about to be put asleep. It was in that moment that I realized how precious life and time is. How fortunate we are and how nothing is guaranteed. How we can be here one moment and gone the next. How mysterious and priceless life is. For that we have to make the most of it and make time for things that matter, which includes our health.

Your health is the most important wealth. You got only one body for this experience of life. Your body is the only place you have to live in. Your body is a gift to your soul. Use it wisely.

Chapter 11

ALIGNMENT WITH THE UNIVERSE

"Shine like the whole universe is yours."

-*Rumi*

What You Are Looking For Is Looking For You

You are searching for happiness and bliss that would last forever. You know deep inside how good and satisfying it feels. You know it exists and it feels so close. You know it would bring healing. You know it would bring warmth to you that would fill your entire body. You know that it would eliminate your stress, anxiety, and fear. You know that feeling so well and you want it so badly. You want more of it. You want it more often. You want to bask in it and never let go. You want it all the time and for that, you engage in a never-ending search for it.

You involve yourself in constant activity in a belief that your happiness and bliss must be out there somewhere. It must be in a different place. It must be with a different person. It must be at a different job, in a different experience. You look for any ways that might possibly bring you to your happiness destination.

You want to go on an exotic vacation. You plan for it. You are so excited that waiting seems impossible. You rush through weeks or even months to arrive at the promised day. You pack the best clothes, the finest shoes, and the most lavish jewelry. You book the most beautiful room with a gorgeous view of the ocean. You plan everything to the last minor detail in order to make the finest getaway ever. When you finally arrive at the place you were looking forward to, you feel the bliss. The air is filled with joy and happiness. You think you have arrived in heaven, and it feels like nirvana.

Your nirvana is the bliss that lured you in, the first hours during the day are amazing. By the end of the day, it gets less exciting. The second day, it starts to fade away and little by little the same feeling of emptiness creeps in. You realize that the bliss lasted only for a day or two. Then, the sun gets too hot so you look for the shade. You spend some time in the shade but then the shade gets too cold. You need to get a blanket. You start being hungry. You order a snack. The snack feels amazing and gets your taste buds going. You order more food until you cannot move. You ate too much. Now you feel too full so you take a nap. You wake up from your nap only to look for the next activity. You are looking for the next excitement. You are searching for the next pleasure. You are in a need of the next amusement.

The excitement never stays permanently nor does it last for a long time. You are always looking for the next, better or newer thing. You are constantly looking for the next source of satisfaction until boredom strikes again. You are restless because you are searching for bliss on the outside. Happiness becomes a destination addiction.

"When I get this new house, when I marry this man, when I get this new promotion, I will be happy," you say to yourself. When the new house comes, you marry the man of your dreams and get your promotion –

but does it satisfy you for long? The excitement lasts for a few months, maybe for a couple of years – but sooner or later, you find yourself on the same journey of pursuit of happiness.

You are back to square one. You are looking for the next happiness, the next excitement, the next bliss. The thing that you were looking for somehow always seems to be out of reach. It seems to be passing you by as you stand there waiting for it. Eventually, you see that you are in a never ending search for the "thing". The quest goes on and you can see no end in sight. As a result, you become anxious and depressed.

Have you ever wondered why forever happiness always seems to be out of reach? Why is it that once you think you have it in your hands, happiness disappears again? The reason is that you attach happiness to the outer, the external. Your happiness becomes conditional on the external environment, an outer experience, or a person other than yourself. This is a very dangerous idea. It is more risky than you realize. Making your happiness dependent on external things, you will never be in control of it. It will always shift. It will always turn. It will always disappear. You will have to start looking for it all over again because you are at the mercy of its whims.

Living In A Bliss

> "Fear is present when we forget that we are a part of God's divine design. Learning to experience authentic love means abandoning ego's insistence that you have much to fear and that you are in an unfriendly world. You can make the decision to be free from fear and doubt and return to the brilliant light of love that is always with you."
>
> *-Wayne Dyer*

The man of your dreams can leave you. You can lose the house you worked so hard to get. You might not get the promotion you think you deserve. It is called life, which is accompanied by ups and downs. Life can turn in so many different ways, which can be in your favor or against you. There are always chances of things going against your expectations and your wishes. This, of course, creates fear in you. Now, you cannot sleep and you are too worried. You buy an insurance policy on the house. You try to please your boss in hopes that you'd get a promotion. You insure your vacation and buy a life insurance but you are still worrying and unable to sleep. The worries and stress is with you through day and night. It is deep inside you because you know there is no guarantee. Life is just happening to you and it's all out of your control. You feel like a puppet on a string.

You live in a state of fear, which has a low vibrational energy. You are not at ease and it reflects on your entire wellbeing. You might not have any immediate disease diagnosis but you feel like you are not at the height of your wellness. You feel like you are not all you could be. You fear the day a medical expert detects your malfunctioning. You are trying to hide while you seek medical experts to confirm that there is nothing wrong. You keep looking for disease instead of health. You are unaware of this desperate search but you are unconsciously looking for 'what you consciously do not want'. It is only a matter of time.

Fear creates energy blockage and you are no longer flowing. When you become stagnant due to this energy block, your body is forced to live in a chronic 'fight-or-flight' mode. Cortisol and adrenaline is released into your system. They affect many crucial bodily functions from digestive, nervous to cardiovascular system and everything in between. Your entire body is in a survival mode. You are no longer at the growth stage. You are no longer in a healing mode where ultimate wellbeing is realized. You are just surviving instead of thriving.

To thrive and heal you have to love and in order to love, you have to let go of fear. You have to let go of your past, which is possible by forgiving the past. Forgive not only yourself but also others that might have hurt you. It is time to forgive everything that had happened to you. Remove yourself from the pain of the past. Access the power of now, the only moment where life exists. It is only in the now, never in any other time. In the present time, in the present moment, you will find your own power. This purifies the pain of the past forever.

You are no longer your past. You are no longer the embodiment of your fear. You are in charge. You are only love and happiness that always existed within you. The only way for you to connect with it is to stop pursuing it. When you stop rushing around and immerse yourself in everything, you will find true bliss. You must immerse yourself in the incredible stillness that is filled with an infinite movement. It is the vortex of energies dancing within yourself. You will realize an abundant beauty and peace everywhere around you.

You need to go beyond the mind. The mind is the instrument fueled by fear. To realize the bliss, you need to rise above your mind. You need to ascend your current state of thinking, analyzing and controlling. Quiet the mind, relax, breathe and just be. Stop trying to control the world because no one can ever control the world. The only world you can control is your inner world. You are the master of your inner world. So, stop judging and focus on bringing peace. Let go of all thoughts and accept things as they are. Do not judge anything as good, bad, better or worse. Just go with the flow and let yourself be a part of the flow. Relax and breathe because you are in good hands; you are loved.

In that moment of surrendering yourself to the flow without judgment, you rise higher. You ascend the mind and unlock your heart, which is the most powerful force in this Universe. Your heart is the divine force of life. It is five thousand times more powerful magnetically and sixty times more powerful electrically than the brain. Imagine the power that you can unleash and become supernatural! It is the lost link between you and everything else. Love can end any kind of war. It can heal any disease. Love has the power to put an end to human suffering. Unconditional love that is eternal is all that you'll ever need.

By letting go of fear and opening the heart, you are open to all your dreams and limitless abundance that is available to you. All that you desire will come, once you become receptive. When you open your heart and start loving without fears and conditions, you tune into the highest vibrational energy possible. This energy will be matched with the same. You will be wrapped in love, the most protective shield. You will return back to love, your natural state of being. You will be love itself and once you are love, you will receive the same. It is the law of attraction; you do not get what you wish for but what you are. When you love, you will see yourself in other beings.

ALIGNMENT WITH THE UNIVERSE

A new world of unlimited potential will open up to you. A world where there is plenty for everyone, there is no need to compete, hate or exploit others. It will teach you how to trust again, wholly and completely. It will erase any doubt in yourself or anything around you. Love is the key. You will become a love magnet yourself. In a state of love, you will realize the supernatural powers within you.

You will find your inner peace in the present moment. You will no longer live through your past. Once you let go of the past, you will not be anxious for the future.

Moreover, you will be complete and fulfilled. You will be still, and in that moment, you will find inner peace. All the answers you were seeking will start coming to you. Without the superficial, self-imposed restrictions, everything will start to make sense. All the suffering and things you could not comprehend before will become clear. You will come out of the position of a victim. You will shed the old skin like a snake. It was old and tight. You have outgrown it. The skin is the old you, which is being shed. Instead of being a powerless prey, you are a warrior now! A warrior who has unleashed his supernatural powers. Nothing can any longer stop you, nor break you down. You found what you have been looking for.

All this time, you have been unknowingly looking for You.

Searching For Gold

> "There are only two ways to live your life. One is as though nothing is a miracle. The other is as though everything is a miracle."
>
> *-Albert Einstein*

What does it mean to give something a name? It means to communicate a description, feeling or to identify yourself with that thing and that feeling. Isn't it?

We call a thing an apple and now we think we know what that apple is. In truth however, we know very little about an apple beyond its color and shape. Our knowing might possibly extend to know how a specific kind of apple tastes and that an apple is possibly healthy. This is how far our typical *knowing* extends. We might not know the fact that there are more than two thousand and five hundred varieties of an apple but that only a crabapple is native to North America. We might not know that apple contains no fat, sodium, or cholesterol and it is a great source of fiber. We might not know that it takes four to five years for an apple tree to produce its first fruit or that apple is a member of the rose family. We might not know that it takes about thirty-six apples to produce one gallon of apple cider.

We might not also know that the science of apple cultivation is known as Pomology. We might also not know that the average person eats sixty-five apples a year and that humans have been consuming apples from as far as 6500BC. In addition, we might not know that apple trees live over one hundred years and that it originated from Kazakhstan. We might not know that most of apple's powerful anti-oxidants include Quercetin, which are found on the skin. Moreover, we may not know that the soluble fiber in an apple is called pectin. Pectin can help an individual lower cholesterol levels. We might not know that unlike the common beliefs that an apple was the forbidden fruit of Eden, it is not mentioned anywhere in the Bible. We might not know that it takes energy from fifty leaves to produce an apple. An average apple has ten seeds containing cyanide that is very toxic. But the tiny amount of poison may pass through our digestive system intact since it is nicely locked away inside the hard seed coat.

We might not know that apple can boost estrogen levels in menopausal women to a great extent. Apple can greatly stimulate electrical activity in the brain and increases mental alertness. We might not know that apple contains high level of boron, which is great to prevent osteoporosis and strengthens bones. People who consume the most apples in the world are Turks. It would also explain why Turkey is among the highest producers of apples in the world. It is also said that people who love apples are to be outspoken, charismatic and enthusiastic.

And we thought we knew an apple! We could spend days, months and even years studying an apple. We could completely immerse ourselves into the world of apple and find astonishing things. These new findings would turn the common apple into one of the most miraculous wonders. But because we label it, apple loses its spark and it becomes a regular thing. I am sure, however, that you might think differently the next time you bite into this delicious fruit of heaven.

We, as a society, are so quick to put a label on a thing, situation and person. Why do we label and judge? The moment we name a thing, we immediately dispose of that thing from any further admiration and potential exploration. The moment we judge, we throw away the deeper truth that exists. It is only available when we start peeling the layers and go deeper into the unknown. We give a label and move onto the next.

Each and every label is associated with a feeling. It is a personal feeling from our past, what kind of recollection we have about the thing we labeled. It is a label from our limited *knowing.*

For example, if as a little child, your mom overreacted whenever there was a bee close by, you will be most likely afraid of bees as you grow up. You will be afraid of getting stung. You will view the bee as a danger. However, if your mom admired the bee and told you how important the creature really is; and that it produces one third of our food supply you will look at the bee as a blessing. Even though, you'll be still aware that you can get stung, you will look at it from a loving rather than fearful and hateful perspective. It is still the same creature with two completely different perspectives. Two completely different perspectives can result in completely different results. One can result in killing the creature whereas the other one will result in protecting the creature. Since this creature provides for one third of our food supply, our judgment can be rather detrimental if we go out and destroy all the bees.

Naming is a useful tool of generalizing and for throwing away things and people. We say they are Buddhists, Christians, Hindus, Germans, or Americans. With a label, you assume you know these people. Now, it is easy to judge and destroy the label. We are taught to believe it is us here and it is *them* there. We are the good ones and the others are bad, evil. We point out to a whole country and say it is the evil that must be destroyed.

I have traveled the world from Libya to China, from China to Japan, from Japan to Switzerland, from Switzerland to Spain, from Spain to Poland, from Poland to Croatia, from Croatia to Mexico and from Mexico to Guatemala. I have never met a country where evil people reside. To the contrary, I met regular people like you and I. They want to see their children safe, enjoy a nice meal with a family and friends.

People who want to live in harmony. None of these people want war or killing. They were kind and loving, same as you and I. They were laughing and crying the same way as you and I do. I have never seen evil in any of them.

The only time I saw evil was when people were politically oppressed for generations, taken advantage of or manipulated through false stories and beliefs into killing other beings. It was only possible because their minds were manipulated and hijacked. Their natural state of being of love was suppressed and replaced by fear. As a result, they were taught to hate.

A country is only an illusionary entity. If you look deeper, you would find that a country is made of people like us. They have the same feelings and emotions. They have the same dreams and wishes. They have families with children like we do. They want to enjoy their life just like we do. They want to be happy same as we do. They want to raise their children and see them prosper like everyone else. They want to enjoy good times and live in peace same as we do. No one wants to be living in a constant state of war and suffering. No parents want to see their children die.

Nationalism teaches us to take credit for something we have not done and hate people we have never met. It teaches us that there is an evil we have to fight so that the good can prevail. Our political leaders tell us to hate and fight people we have never even met. Those people have not done anything to us. We were just told a story that we blindly believe and send our children to kill other children.

When you do not label people, you are forced to know them on a personal level. You need to know the individual. Giving a label is to deny, condemn, and justify. Without a label, you cannot do this. When there is no label, there is a sense of nothing and you cannot destroy nothing. Without labeling and judging, there is a transformation of the mind. The mind becomes tranquil and everything comes into being with all its infinite potentials. It takes a conscious focus and everyday practice to stop judging and labeling. When we judge and label, it is a reflection of our fears. We have been taught to do this since our childhood through cultural conditioning. We are not even aware of our beliefs that create the lens through which we see the world. It is our mind creating its own opinion on things, people, and situations. Our mind and its thoughts create our reality. What we think, we become. If we think positive thoughts, we are positive. If we think negative thoughts, we are negative. Negative mind can never create a positive reality.

We need to stop our brain from playing games on us. We need to upgrade our neuro circuitry and ascent from a state of fear to a state of life. We need to upgrade our subconscious programming. If you do not want to be sick, you have to stop thinking like a sick patient. You have to start thinking like a healthy person. You have to focus on your health and vitality rather than analyzing and looking for a disease.

There is a need to break the vicious cycle and get out of the negative programming. You need to re-train your brain to stop labeling and judging. You have to train it to see the good in everything. It is the Yin and Yang philosophy being applied. Yin and Yang is an ancient Chinese concept where all things exist as inseparable and contradictory opposites such as day-night, male-female, and young-old. The two opposites attract each other and each of it has at its core an element of the counterpart. Neither one of them is better or worse. They both bring a balance in order to achieve harmony. Everything bad has something good and everything good has some bad in it as well. We need to zoom in and bring the good out of every situation. It is that simple, yet so powerful practice. When things happen just accept them as is. Do not try to form an immediate opinion about it. Give it a moment and then try to look for the good.

ALIGNMENT WITH THE UNIVERSE

Like any new things you start learning in life, it might be hard at the beginning. Think of this like you're learning a new language. It will take focus, practice, and dedication. It will take a lot of repetition because you will train the mind to see differently. It has to memorize new instructions. The ego will fight you at first because of its deeply rooted habits. Nonetheless, practice makes you the master. With time, you will see the good in everything and eventually this will become a habit. A habit of trusting and believing that everything happens for a reason. A habit of trusting and believing that we are in good hands because the Universe has our back.

Learn how to forgive because we all make mistakes. Only when we go searching for the deeper truth, we might see the full picture. Judging because of our immediate reaction to the situation will only lead you astray. Take your time to search for the complete truth so that you can fully understand the situation or person. This is vital to find the much-needed compassion and love to forgive. Forgiveness is the biggest gift to yourself. We all want to be understood, forgiven, and fully appreciated. We all want to matter. The truth is, we already matter, no matter what.

Trust in all there is. Trust that you are the same as others. Trust in your originality and vulnerability that will create a bridge between you and others. Learn how to see yourself in others. Look for the good in yourself and others. See yourself and all the mistakes you have done. You were given another chance and even if you were not, this is your time to show the world different way of being without judging and labeling.

What You Resist Persists

"The intensity of the pain depends on the
degree of resistance to the present moment."

-*Eckhart Tolle*

I have had a lot of struggles most of my life. My entire life seemed like one big struggle. I was constantly fighting with something. My entire existence was one big push. The problems to deal with did not have an end. When one issue at work resolved, there was another one to arise. When the fridge got fixed the car broke down. When one bill got paid another unexpectedly arrived. Life was very stressful with no relief in sight. Life was a struggle.

As a working mom, I had many hats to wear. I did not like most of the things I had to do. If it was not things around the children, it was things around the house. If it was not things around the house, it was things around my work. If it was not things around my work, it was things around my parents. My chores were endless. I turned my life into one big mêlée because of it.

When we started our family business there were thousands of other things to do. I had to do things I had no interest in. There were things I had no prior experience with. I did not care to do these tasks. One of them was accounting. I despised to be buried for hours in endless numbers. It was not my cup of tea. It was taking me away from what I loved to do. I wanted to be creative and focus on other things. I was not into it. It was taking my precious time from helping others heal into crunching numbers and producing reports.

The subject was confusing. I could not figure it out. It was difficult because I decided that I do not like it. I had much more important job to do. I created a negative perception that lead into a resistance. I created self-imposed limitation that I do not like accounting. My mind decided it is not fun and for that it was no fun. With that, I resisted to learn anything about it to make the job any easier. When time came to do the numbers, I had the mindset to hate the experience. I'd tell myself, *"You can be doing something better right now. You are wasting your precious time with meaningless numbers."* I programmed myself for having a bad time. I created an inner battle in that very moment by judging the experience.

The more I thought about disliking it, the more I struggled with it. The more I was not liking it, the more difficult it was. Then one day, I became tired of having a bad time. Something had to change. I knew that I still have to do it but I also knew I can turn the experience around somehow. I had to change my perception towards it. I had to change my thinking. I had to change my mind. I decided that I am going to enjoy the job.

I made myself a nice cup of green tea. I turned my favorite meditation music on. I set my mind to have a good time. I read some tips and researched the accounting software I was using. I started to experiment with it. I found some great tips to make the job easier. I applied what I learned. I also made a mental note that I will find something good in the task.

The first time was not easy. I had to remind myself to enjoy it. I had a hard time. It did not feel natural. I had to force myself not to judge. I had to remind myself it will get better. The second time was less difficult. The third time things were easier.

By the fifth time, I noticed a major shift. I was actually having fun. I was actually looking forward to my accounting *therapy*. Hard to believe! What happened was a shift of my consciousness. I dropped my inner resistance. I dropped my fear. I dropped my judgment. It was still the same accounting but what changed was my inner fight with it. It was an incredible discovery. I started to look at the numbers from a completely different prospective. I started to look at it with an interest. I wanted to see what the numbers actually meant. I made astonishing discoveries once I zoomed in. I found out that we are spending too much in certain areas. I discovered that we are not spending enough in other areas. I was able to dive deep into our business once I let go of my inner resistance. I was able to make fantastic adjustments that resulted in savings and better profits.

It was like winning a battle. I have applied the same technique to other things in my life. I discovered amazing powers in this simple exercise. I learned a magic trick how to turn pain into joy. Becoming conscious and fully aware of your inner fears is a path to awakening.

Awakening is not an escape from your everyday life and pain. It is an understanding of your suffering. Awakening will make you see. Awakening will make you understand. Awakening will make you connect. It will provide the needed liberation from you daily pain. It is through the understanding of your suffering where your pain will disappear. You will become content with whatever you are doing. You will be fully conscious and aware of yourself.

Contentment through awakening cannot leave you. If your joy and pleasure comes and goes it is not a real contentment. It is just a disparity between one moment of pleasure and another. This is not a real contentment. Anything that comes and goes is an illusionary joy. It is not real. It is entertainment. It is merely an amusement to keep you busy. It is diversion from having to face yourself.

You were born excited. You were born thrilled. Excitement is natural. Life itself is excitement until you were told otherwise. It was not until the society took your excitement and made you miserable. Only miserable people can be manipulated and controlled. Only miserable people can be told to give themselves for the sake of better life after this one. Only miserable people can be put into a hamster wheel with a promise of nirvana somewhere else. Only miserable people can be told that they have to die in order to go to heaven.

Excited people cannot be controlled. They cannot be manipulated. They know their true value and who they are. Excited people know they were born into heaven. They found heaven right here in this life time. Awakened people are dangerous to the society. They cannot be conformed. These people cannot be enslaved.

Life is not difficult. Life is fun. Life is a playful journey. It is only your inner struggle leading to a resistance. Where attention goes, energy flows. It is the law of physics.

Self-Doubt

"Courage is knowing what not to fear."

-Plato

My friend Kate decided to get her driver's license. I was still living in former Czechoslovakia. It was an expensive, rigid process that lasted for eight weeks. It cost an entire one month's salary. It was a serious commitment.

Kate never finished her driver's license. The process consisted of written test, followed by a series of driving tests. The written test was no problem. She mastered the learning process. She knew how to memorize facts in order to take tests. She was a brilliant student. She was great at memorizing. However, the driving portion was an issue. It was during one of her driving tests, when she was sitting with her instructor and they entered an intersection. My friend completely froze. Her brain was overloaded with information. She could not handle the pressure.

There were pedals to push. There was steering wheel to manage. There were gears to shift. There was an instructor yelling at her. There were traffic lights to watch for. There were other cars on the road. There were pedestrians. It was too much for her to process. She did not know how to handle. She completely panicked. She was with her instructor at the middle of an intersection. She stopped the car, opened the door and walked out of the running car right there. She gave up. My friend Kate never completed her driver's license nor drove a car again.

This is a great example of how overpowering a new experience can be and the fear arising from the unknown. When you are learning something new you are creating new set of instructions that will be eventually programmed into the subconscious part of the brain with time. It takes repetition and practice to make it a habit in order to become good at the new practice. This is due to the limitations of the conscious mind.

The conscious mind is one million times less powerful processor then the subconscious mind. When you are learning something new you have to be very alert and pay attention. You are venturing out of your comfort zone. You are creating new experience through which you are creating new neuron connections. It consumes a lot of energy and focus.

There are times where such an experience can be overwhelming. The limited conscious processor might not be able to handle too many operations going on at the same time. It is a situation where fear comes in and takes over the situation. That was the case of my friend's driving experience. Her subconscious mind did not know enough about driving a car yet. It was a gray area of unknown. It was a data overload. Her inner fear of the unknown took over. It was unfamiliar area. Self doubt fueled by fear took over. My friend Kate could not process the multitude of operations happening at the same time. She gave up. She surrendered to fear.

Self-doubt happens when you fear the unknown. When you start questioning your ability to do something you have not done before. Fear can only rise when we label and judge. You judge a certain situation that it might be something you cannot do. You are projecting a label without true understanding. It is your opinion about the situation that creates self-doubt. It is your idea. It is your lack of experience. It is a lack of knowledge of the fact that creates fear.

The moment you give something a name or label you create fear. Labeling and naming carries the unknown. The moment you examine the same thing without labeling that feeling disappears. It fades away. You can be completely free of fear when you stop putting images, symbols, judgments or names. It is a process of getting to know yourself. It is a process of self-knowledge. Self-knowledge is a path to your wisdom. Wisdom is the end of fear.

Resistance

"Life itself is the most wonderful fairy tale."
-*Hans Christian Anderson*

Greek half-God Sisyphus was punished to meaninglessly push a boulder up the mountain, only to have it roll it back down again. Nobel Prize winning author, Albert Camus took the story of Sisyphus as a metaphor to describe the struggle of humanity. He questioned how we can find the meaning in our existence. It is our human nature to continue building endlessly for the future that never arrives, and then we die. We constantly stress and fear challenges and anything that goes against our perception of pleasure.

Life is everything but what our fear-programmed mind imagines. Life is not difficult nor struggle. We take life too seriously. We turned life into such a drama. We turned life into a corporate agreement with terms and conditions. We have been culturally programmed for possibilities that things will not go as planned. We have been programmed into fear and scarcity. We allowed fear to run our life.

Life is not difficult at all. Life is quite the opposite. Life is easy. Life is playful. Life is joyful. Life is full of magic. Life is fun. It is all the rules that want you to remain contained. The rules want you scared and think small. Going by the rules and limitations will surely turn anything into one small box of a tight confinement. If you follow the rules you will miss all the fun. Life will feel like pushing a large boulder up a hill.

Think about it for a moment. Look at your life. Look at your thoughts. Go deep inside your mind to make a notice. Try to understand what Sisyphus tried to portray. After a good review and deep analysis you will find out that it is you who is making things much harder for yourself. It is you who is creating resistance in certain areas of your life because of your own perceptions. You are only doing it because you are judging. You are judging things between good and bad.

The power is in your judgment. It creates a perception that things are difficult. Your mind makes you think that things are hard. That things are not possible. From there, resistance is born. It is you and your judgment that is applying a power to things you do not like. It is bringing it alive. You are the Sisyphus of your life.

ALIGNMENT WITH THE UNIVERSE

The first step to correct your hardship is your judgment. You need to learn not to judge. You need to accept things you cannot change and change things you cannot accept. The second step is to find beauty in everything. No matter how hard or difficult things seem to appear there is always something good in everything. Look for the good. Look for the blessing. Look for the lesson you are suppose to learn. It is there. You just need to be patient and learn how to see. You will have to practice this on daily basis. You will need to be living in the moment, fully aware and conscious of everything around you including your thoughts. Any negative thought you will have to stop right in its tracks.

Think of it but do not judge it. Do not give it a label. Then try to immediately replace it with a positive perception of the situation. It will require concentration. It will require inner work. With time this will become your practice. You will retrain your brain. You will upgrade your programming. Once you master this it will be a major battle won. Your entire life will change. Your entire world will transform.

It will be as if someone removed dark glasses from your eye sight. It is your perception of the world that will change. With your changed perception everything else will change. You will no longer push things. You will allow things that crash to crash. You will allow things that work to work. You will no longer stress over things you cannot change. You will learn how to flow with life. You will have fun in anything you do. It can be anything from washing dishes, cleaning floor, creating sales presentation or preparing financial statements. The activity will no longer matter because there will no longer be any resistance applied.

The moment you change your attitude you drop the inner resistance. When you adopt attitude of gratitude you will rise your altitude. Instead of feeling the weight of the entire world on your shoulders, you will enjoy everything around you. Being in harmony and thankful is the way to reach the top.

The closer you will be coming to yourself, the closer you will be to the Universe. It will be the greatest moment when you accept the mystery of this world. It will be a moment when you stop questioning and start trusting in life as a wholesome process of our existence. It is the mysterious and beyond any knowledge. You will accept that while you seek knowledge the Universe will remain forever mysterious.

Judgment

> "Real magic in relationships means an absence of judgment of others."
>
> -*Wayne Dyer*

Many people noticed when I awakened from the years of social programming and hypnosis. They noticed that I am different. Many asked me to be *normal*. I looked at them and smiled. *"I have tried to be normal most of my life. It was the worst time ever."*

What does it mean to be normal? What is normal? Does it mean to be like everyone else? That does not sound normal. It seems extremely abnormal. It is an insult to your soul. It is an abuse of your spirit. Normal is a lie! There is no such thing as normal.

Nothing is until you compare it with something else. It is the law of relativity. What's normal to a spider is chaos to the fly! Some people think that spending leisure time on a sofa in front of TV is normal while others would consider it is an absolute waste of time. Some people think it is normal to be sick while others would think it is absolutely abnormal. Some people think it is normal to go drinking after work every day while others consider it rather unhealthy.

ALIGNMENT WITH THE UNIVERSE

What some consider normal in one part of the world might sound completely strange, weird or even horrifying in another. In United States, we put our child's tooth underneath the pillow and exchange it for hard cash from a tooth fairy. In Greece, parents throw their baby's tooth on their roof. In Spain, male residents of a small Northern community dress up as the devil and jump over infants who are laid on mattresses along the street. It is called El Colacho and is to keep the devil away. In South Korea, people avoid using red ink to write someone's name. It is believed that red ink was used to write down names of dead people based on their history and customs.

In the Satare Mawe tribe in Brazil, boys become men by proving their bravery. They have to show their courage by placing hands in a basket filled with angry bullet ants. When the bullet ants bite it is the most excruciating pain. In Lopburi in Thailand, people provide fruit and vegetable feast for local monkeys. Monkeys are atop a buffet table feasting on thousands of kilograms of scrumptious meals. In Spain, La Tomatina is the largest tomato fight in the world. It is quite an abnormal custom among Valencians in Bunol to use tomatoes as weapons.

In Muslin countries, women from the bride's family paint designs on the bride's feet. It is to indicate womanhood, bring fertility and good luck to the bride. In Tanomani tribe in Venezuela, when a person dies the body is cremated. The bone ashes are made into a soup that is consumed by the people attending the ceremony. It is believed it preserves the deceased spirit and provides a resting place in their bodies. In China, brides living in Wuling Mountains cry for a month as a part of their wedding preparations. They have been also putting young girls through a painful foot binding process.

For almost thousand years, Chinese people believed that small feet were attributes of beauty and sex appeal. This belief made Chinese men and women to intentionally restrict the feet from growing bigger by binding them. This was stopped only in the 1940's as it was recognized as debilitating experience imposed on young Chinese girls. In the rural areas of India there is a festival worshiping snakes. People carry snakes in pots placed on their heads while dancing to music. Some of the most venomous snakes are used including cobras.

There are thousands upon thousands of unique traditions, customs and interesting activities people engage in. There are millions upon millions different things humans can think of as their *normal* way while the other way would be rather abnormal. It is only to demonstrate that normal does not exist. It is only subjective reasoning what you might consider within a certain norm of your cultural, political, or religious upbringing. We all are unique and rather peculiar beings. You are an individual until you were gathered into a certain crowd. You have very unique way about you. Every other person is exactly the same way unique as you. Everyone is unique in their own unique way.

Each and every single person could literally start their own culture, belief and political party. For that you cannot judge. You shall not condemn something that is not your own way of being. It is what makes us so beautiful and unique.

Working The Magic

"Life would be tragic if weren't funny."
-*Stephen Hawking*

Besides making miracles happen within the area of health there were also many other great areas in my life where miracles started to show up. Like the time when I forgot my ID and flew to a conference on my Costco card instead. It was an early Monday morning and I was rushing. I left my driver's license at home. I found out as I was standing in a security line at the airport. My heart dropped. I had to make the flight leaving in one hour. If it was in the past I would be completely stressed out. I would turn the situation into a disaster. I would be combative and resist what was happening fearing negative outcome.

This time I knew there is no point. It is what it is. I had to turn on my super powers. I accepted my mistake. I smiled. I explained what happened and asked the people at the security for forgiveness. I asked if they can help me. I thanked them in advance. I was humble and hoping they will feel my sincerity. If they could not I would understand. It was no one else's fault but mine. I was sending love to the situation. Amazingly, everyone came to my rescue. The authorities were regular people like me. They could see themselves in me. They all came together to ensure I made my flight without any issue. It was a miracle that I made my flight and my conference.

Life is ten percent what happens to us and ninety percent how we respond to it. It is that simple. Things will happen no matter how hard you try. It is very easy to turn situations into an issue by being demanding and blame others. It does not help you. It provides no relief. On the contrary, you are creating resistance that will be a painful process. It will be stressful process. It will be unhealthy process affecting your physical wellness.

Learn the trick how to always feel good on the inside. Learn how to be in charge of the situation by the way you feel. It is all up to you. It is a simple three-step process.

First: Own your mistake.
Second: Admit it.
Third: Ask for forgiveness.

Ask for help. Don't be afraid to be vulnerable. Be accepting of the situation. That is all that it takes. Practice it. Be patient and watch miracles appearing in your life.

When you show vulnerability, you are taking your mask down. You are showing your real self. You are displaying a real human being. You are showing your love. It is a sacred language that connects you with everyone else. People unconsciously speak this language from the moment they were born. It is a language of miracles.

No one is perfect. Everyone makes mistakes. You forget driver license. You make wrong decision. You are tired and snap. You are not the nicest because you are having a bad day. It will happen, no matter how much you try. It happens because we are humans. We are not robots. Please do remember this crucial difference. You came here to learn from your mistakes and to do better. We all did and so will the generations after us.

Life is filled with ups and downs. Knowing how to navigate through both, the good and less good days, is a true art. You are in full charge of it. It is a matter of owning your actions and being responsible. Or you can be in denial and be a victim. When you decide for the first you keep control. You are always in charge of the way you feel. When you decide to be a victim you surrender your powers to others. You literally give them power over you. You give them the power to decide how they will make you feel.

Entitlement

> "A sense of entitlement is a cancerous thought process and void of gratitude which can be deadly to our relationships."
>
> -*Steven Maraboli*

We live in such an abundant and plentiful world. There is more than we could ever need and yet we are rushing through life like we need to be somewhere else. We are rushing around like we need to attain something more. This constant search, constant desire and constant need makes us lose touch with the realization over how much we have and how blessed we are. This disconnect creates a void and feeling of lack. It makes us feel how much more we deserve and should receive from everyone. People have been conditioned into this unhealthy belief wherever you look. We have been conditioned into a state of scarcity.

The conditioning comes from our environment. It is the TV telling you what you need to buy. The social media dictates how you should look. Every other marketing channel is there to make you feel *how little you have* and *how little you are.* It is a clever scheme to always make you feel incomplete. To further entice your shopping appetite, there is also the bright idea of putting a sale on things that you do not need. Not because you already have a full garage filled with similar junk. They do this to make you feel like you need the exact thing they are trying to sell.

It is not your fault because you have been programmed into this type of thinking. This faulty thinking is very beneficial to the business and our society. It is a brilliantly constructed design of enslavement. It is a seemingly innocent design and you are not even aware of it. You cannot detect anything wrong because the system is not broken, it was intentionally designed this way. The design is supposed to turn unique, beautiful souls into empty, mindless consumers.

Consumers whose only mission is to consume because they never know when they have had enough. It is the constant need feeding our hungry ego structure. Its hunger is only getting bigger because there is so much more you can have, especially in a place such as the United States. It is the land of plenty and the land of devastating waste. We have created such diseased consumer minds that people are shopping nonstop. It became the pastime and addictive hobby of the new century. And it is now spreading like a plague across the rest of the globe.

For the entire week, people shop for the latest shoes, fashion, technological gadgets, knickknacks, house décor, cars, boats and the list is endless. There is so much to shop for, especially with the invention of the best shop ever – the Internet! It is open twenty four seven and never runs out of supply. It is a shopping paradise for lost souls. Shopping has become such a dangerously addictive affair. It never stops nor does your desire to have more.

Most people do not even know what they are shopping for. As long as they are getting a good deal, they will continue shopping. Many times, it is not even about the actual item but rather about saving money. Saving money has become such a pride, hasn't it? Getting a good deal is very important to everyone because wasting money would be a sin.

The fact that you are buying a t-shirt for three dollars, shoes for ten and lunch for four does not raise any questions at all. How is it possible that someone can actually produce products and especially food that cheap? While everyone, including you, feels like their hourly rate should be well over that amount? There is no free lunch. There is always price for everything.

ALIGNMENT WITH THE UNIVERSE

Cheap is expensive! Somewhere, some place, somehow someone is taking advantage of someone or something in order to get you shoes made for ten dollars, a meal for four and free spa treatment. It can be the shoe factory in Indonesia, which is not keeping their building up to a code and people burn in masses because of the unsafe work environment. Or someone is loading your food with toxic deadly preservatives so it can last on the shelf for weeks and months. Or it is the mass agriculture feeding antibiotics to their animals for bigger profits. Eventually that toxic food will only make you sick at the end.

Similarly, someone in India is polluting the Earth's rivers with all the color dyes that force local people to flee. The local spa needs to close because it cannot afford to survive on discounted services. It is when we just don't look at things but start looking through things we see a deeper truth. We usually turn our head away and pretend like it has nothing to do with us. It is none of our wrong doing, we are not responsible for any of this. Instead of taking any responsibility, we blame others for our global crisis. What we miss to see is that by being part of our never-ending shopping needs, we are the problem itself. Demand only feeds the supply. We are so disconnected from reality and each other.

Running my own small business was one of the biggest eye opening lessons. Going through the experience myself, I understood what conducting business actually requires of an individual who wants to bring honest service to others. It is nothing like working for a large corporation going in everyday to do the job.

Contrarily, running a small business is about creating these jobs and keeping the lights on. Most people have absolutely no idea how business is created and how it functions effectively. I was one of those people, until I started my own company. It is a never-ending job. I had to constantly worry about the market, bringing customers, hiring good employees, keeping them motivated, caring for the business, ensuring there was enough money in the bank to pay the bills, keeping customers happy, keeping up with the competition, keeping state and federal compliances and a million other things.

It was pure labor of love, especially when you never get to see a paycheck at the end of the day. There was no such a thing as going home at 6pm, relaxing or having a weekend off. The work never stopped nor could your brain ever completely shut off. The worry was twenty four seven. Our economy was built on a small business once. It was the mom and pops shops where people knew each other and cared for each other. The small business was about providing an honest product and honest service. It was about being a family.

The business owners would never dare to put dangerous chemicals into their product to become rich. They would never dare to cheat for their own benefit. They would not use dangerous poisons nor other tricks because they did not have to. Their customers appreciated their service and they were happy to pay a full price. They cared for the business to stay in business because it provides a service to the community. It was a mutual collaboration and a harmonious relationship. It was a communion where no one needed to exploit each other. It was an energy exchange between conscious beings. It was about being a union. It was about being one.

A small business is no longer a part of the business culture today. It is all about money and quick profits now. Business has become a matter of exploitation. We exploit not only each other but the rest of the world as well. Strong countries like America, Germany, or Japan exploit inferior countries in Africa, South America or Asia. We became the super power of the poor. We might be rich on the outside but we are poor on the inside. Our needs and entitlement is endless. Economic globalization was not designed with some loving intentions in mind. It was designed only to benefit highly industrialized countries while others become inferior. It is about world domination through greed and inequality in wealth distribution.

It can never bring anything positive to the world. It can only lead to starvation, conflict and war over precious resources. We have been gifted with a beautiful planet that has been continually giving and loving. This planet has, however, limited resources, which will eventually run out. Our current benefits and luxuries are only against the disadvantages of someone else. Only a handful of people control fifty percent of the world's resources. This creates a struggle for power. Struggle for power leads to a conflict and conflict can only lead into a war. War creates a separation from the heart.

Society does not want you to be connected with your heart. Society only needs minds, which can be manipulated, controlled, and programmed. Minds are borrowed knowledge. Our society is an establishment of the mind. It is dominated by the mind because it can be maneuvered by greed. Only the mind can turn a human into a machine. Only machines can be motivated and abducted by money and greed. On the other hand, heart is complete, free from greed and money.

Heart cannot be manipulated because it is yours. Nor could the heart be programmed because it is your true self. Your heart is the original version. It makes you powerful and free from fear. Your heart is thousand times more powerful than the mind.

Heart only produces love, which is the most powerful force of this Universe. Love is the source of life. The heart cannot be controlled by egoistic pursuits nor can it be corrupted by money or greed. Heart is the entrance to your supernatural.

Entitlement is a lack of gratitude. It blinds you from recognizing what you have. It makes you believe that you don't have enough. Entitlement feeds your ego construct. Entitlement is deadly to your relationships. It will always make you feel as a victim. It will always make you need to get ahead of someone. It will make you need to gain. It will make you need to own to satisfy the feeling of inner emptiness. Entitlement will never bring you to the magical world of abundance nor will it bring the desired inner peace.

Chose heart over mind. Chose love over fear. Be a person of love, gratitude, and appreciation.

Rise higher to unlock the miraculous powers within you.

About the Author

Transformational coach and spiritual teacher, Lenka Koloma, was born into a doctor family in a small town outside of former communist Czechoslovakia near a German border. Lenka suffered with many health and mental issues since a little child. She was on a search to find meaning and purpose in her life. She thought that living the American dream would deliver that. She worked very hard her entire life to achieve a great material success to only find more suffering. Her professional career only took her into a deeper darkness of inner emptiness. This eventually pushed her into a fight for her own life bringing the needed awakening and enlightenment we are all searching for.

Lenka offers unique expertise in the science of life. Having have to deal with debilitating chronic disease she understands the erroneous approach of trying to find a cure rather than stop the root cause of a disease. Lenka's practice is based on the law of cellular biology and principles of mind-body-spirit homeostasis. It is designed to support body's natural power to heal & repair and stop disease at its root rather then creating a short term patch through drugging with debilitating side effects.

Lenka has traveled throughout Asia, Central America and Europe seeking holistic practices and techniques. She is self-studied in the field of nutritional science, toxicology, physiology and science of life. Her revolutionary detox protocol has helped thousands to heal themselves from chronic conditions such as diabetes, heart disease, thyroid disease, arthritis, cancer and many other health issues. It is Lenka's life-long passion to empower others on their own healing journey and awakening.

Made in the USA
Las Vegas, NV
06 May 2022